TONIGHT'S TOP 20

1. LONG LIVE LOVE   Sandie Shaw
2. A WORLD OF OUR OWN   The Seekers
3. THE CLAPPING SONG   Shirley Ellis
4. POOR MAN'S SON   The Rockin' Berries
5. WHERE ARE YOU NOW   Jackie Trent
6. TRAINS & BOATS & PLANES   Burt Bacharach
6. THE PRICE OF LOVE   Everly Brothers
6. TRUE LOVE WAYS   Peter & Gordon
8. CRYING IN THE CHAPEL   Elvis Presley
9. THIS LITTLE BIRD   Marianne Faithfull
10. KING OF THE ROAD   Roger Miller
11. MARIE   The Bachelors
12. TICKET TO RIDE   The Beatles
13. SUBTERRANEAN HOMESICK BLUES   Bob Dylan
14. NOT UNTIL THE NEXT TIME   Jim Reeves
15. TRAINS & BOATS & PLANES   Billy J. Kramer/Dakota
    Hollies   Françoise Hardy

TOP OF THE POPS
50ᵀᴴ ANNIVERSARY

Patrick Humphries & Steve Blacknell

MᶜNIDDER & GRACE

Dedication

This book is dedicated to our wives and families.

Published by McNidder & Grace
Bridge Innovation Centre,
Pembrokeshire Science and Technology Park,
Pembroke Dock
SA72 6UN

First Published in 2014
© Patrick Humphries and Steve Blacknell 2014
ISBN: 9780857160522

A catalogue record for this work is available from the British Library.
Designed by Obsidian Design
Front cover concept and design by David Muse
Front jacket BBC *TOTP* logos: 1973–86 and 1993–2003 (in the TV)
Back jacket illustration: David Bowie

Picture credits
McNidder & Grace would like to thank the following for permission to reproduce copyright material. While every effort has been made to trace and acknowledge all copyright holders, we would like to apologise for any errors or omissions.
All b/w images are © Harry Goodwin except p.x which is © Simon Atterbury, pp.13, 181 which are © Ron Howard and pp. 96, 132, 150, 170 and 179 which are © BBC.
All colour photos are © BBC.

Printed and bound in Slovenia on behalf of Latitude Press Limited.

Acknowledgements

Special thanks to Stanley Dorfman and Stanley Appel – two of the greats.

Alan Jones and Dave McAleer; Spencer Leigh and Jon Kutner, as ever, provided invaluable information about the UK charts... John Sugar really helped us out of a jam on the technology front... Dick Fiddy was a mine of information about the programme's missing episodes, and all manner of TV matter.

Shaun Tilley stepped up to bat by letting us hear the tapes of interviews he conducted for his own series, *Top of the Pops Playback*. Thanks to Shaun for letting us draw on his interviews with Bruno Brookes, Paul Jordan, Pete Murray, Dixie Peach, Andy Peebles, Mike Read, Dave Lee Travis and Johnnie Walker.

Special thanks to Eddi Fiegel for her illuminating chapter on the show's influence on youth fashion – and to little Georgie, who did her very best to distract Eddi from the job in hand!

And of course the legendary Fred Dellar – not just for the crossword, but for a lifetime of much-loved writing about every aspect of popular music, during which he has brought equal enthusiasm to Swedish death metal and Francis Albert Sinatra. A well-deserved tip of the fedora for Fred...

Harry Goodwin, the official *Top of the Pops* photographer died aged 89 just as this book was completed; Harry's iconic images were an integral part of the programme.

All interviews, unless otherwise stated, were conducted specifically for this book.

The authors also extend fulsome thanks and appreciation to the following:
Kate Adam (& Fraser & Megan...) * Keith Altham * Ian Anderson www.iananderson.com * Rick Astley www.rickastley.co.uk * Simon Atterbury * Louis Barfe www.louisbarfe.com * Dave Bartram www.showaddywaddy.net * Eric Bell * Johnny Beerling www.johnnybeerling.com * Maggie Blacknell * Gary Brooker www.procolharum.com * Paul Burnett * Anna Chamberlain * Jeff Christie www.yellowriver.0catch.com * Steve Collier * Alec Cormack www.attadale.com * John Coughlan www.johncoughlan.com *

Dave Cousins www.strawbsweb.co.uk * Helen Dann * Steve Davis *
Carol Decker www.tpau.co.uk * Bobby Elliott www.hollies.co.uk *
Steve Ellis www.steveellis.co.uk * David Essex www.davidessex.com *
Richard ("The Plumber") Evans * Andy Fairweather-Low
www.andyfairweatherlow.com * Fish www.fish-thecompany.com *
Mo Foster www.mofoster.com * Bill Fowler * Maurice Gallagher *
Denise Goodwin * Graham Gouldman www.grahamgouldman.info *
Paul Green * David Hamilton www.davidhamilton.eu *
Gordon Haskell www.gordonhaskell.com * Dave Hill * Tania Hogan *
Noddy Holder www.noddyholder.com * Neil Innes www.neilinnes.org *
Allan James * David Jensen * Leee John www.imaginationband.com *
Junior www.juniorgiscombe.co.uk * Linda Lewis www.lindalewis.co.uk *
Mark Lewisohn www.marklewisohn.net * Dennis Locorriere
www.dennislocorriere.com * Lem Lubin * Annabella Lwin www.annabellalwin.com *
John McCoy * Sue Menhenick www.panspeople.com * Bernard Newnham *
Gary Numan www.numan.co.uk * Gilbert O'Sullivan www.gilbertosullivan.net *
John Otway www.johnotway.com * Sue Parr ** Nigel Planer
www.nigelplaner.co.uk * Peter Powell * Mark Radcliffe * Maggie Reilly
www.maggiereilly.co.uk * Sir Cliff Richard www.cliffrichard.org * Adrian Sear *
Pat Sharp www.patsharp.co.uk * Rod Smallwood * Andy Peden Smith *
Brian Southall * David Stark www.songlink.com * Alvin Stardust
www.alvinstardust.com * Shaun Tilley www.shauntilley.co.uk * Judy Totton
www.judytotton.com * Midge Ure www.midgeure.com * Dominic Walker *
Pete Waterman www.pwl-empire.com * Chris Welch * Alan Whitehead *
Sir Terry Wogan www.terrywogan.com * Steve Wright

CONTENTS

Cliff Richard – now Sir Cliff and proud holder of the record for most Top of the Pops *appearances*

Foreword
by Sir Cliff Richard

Top of the Pops was always a 'must do'. With all the new technology available today, people forget just how few television outlets there were for rock & roll back when the programme began. But my career had been going for 6 years before that first show was broadcast in 1964!

In its early years, the power of *Top of the Pops* was such that if you performed on the programme, your song was guaranteed to climb up the next week's charts. And at the beginning you had to travel up to Manchester to appear on the show, where you'd meet all the new acts like the Who, the Kinks and the Rolling Stones. On occasion, I even found myself lending a helping hand to more established names – like the Shadows!

I loved doing the *Pops* because you knew that you would be rubbing shoulders with other singers who had been Number One, or were heading that way. You never knew who you were going to bump into – over the years I appeared alongside everyone from the Wurzels to the Police, and Barry Manilow to Jethro Tull!

While the programme itself is now gone, you can still relive those classic moments on the internet and BBC 2. Though, if pressed, my vote would still be to bring *Top of the Pop*s back to our television screens, where it belongs. But if that doesn't happen, then this 50th anniversary book, will tell you all you need to know about a genuine television institution. Remember though: *Top of the Pops* was always more than just a programme; it reflected an era when the charts were vitally important to music. And every week, when that announcement finally came: "It's Number One! It's *Top of the Pops...*", it really meant something... Nowadays, the programme may have gone, but thanks to books like this, those memories live on...

Sir Cliff Richard
London, 2013

The show must go on: Original TOTP *producers Stanley Dorfman (left), and Stanley Appel, frame Leo Sayer, London, 2013*

Stanley Dorfman
Top of the Pops Co-creator, Producer and Director

I joined *Top of the Pops* from the design department, just after Johnnie Stewart started Bill Cotton's brilliant concept of a pop show geared to the combined weekly charts of the *Melody Maker*, *New Musical Express* and BBC radio's own chart .

The rules were that we would only feature singles that were in the top 30.

Only singles that were moving *up* the chart (even if the Beatles dropped from No. 1 to No. 2, even though they were pencilled in for the next show, we had to call Brian Epstein and say 'Sorry mate, but the boys are out!')

We had a 'Tip for the Top', which allowed us to feature new and unknown acts.

And a 'New Release', which featured major acts with a new record.

This format stayed, I believe, for all the years of *TOTP*.

It made the show always fresh, but also extremely difficult as we planned next week, when the charts came out, the day before the live show. There was always a frantic rescheduling: booking and rebooking, pre-recording of acts (particularly visiting Americans) that might be advancing up the chart the following weeks.

Also our brilliant choreographer, Flick Colby, might have to re-plan, reconstruct and re-dress an entirely new routine for the wonderful Pan's People, who each week would dance to an act that was unavailable but strong in the charts.

That said, working on this show was an absolute joy! The excitement of a live show with cameras and cranes pushing their way through a dancing audience of over-enthusiastic teens; the rush of working with performers like the Rolling Stones, the Who, the Kinks, 'Little' Stevie Wonder, the Beach Boys, Supremes, Jimi Hendrix... And of course, the Beatles as well as Dusty, Lulu, Elton and Bowie who were just beginning massive careers.

Who can forget the excitement of John Lennon's first live appearance after the Beatles on the show with 'Instant Karma'? And George Harrison's first appearance with the classic 'My Sweet Lord'.

And the many lifelong friends I made: Ian Ralfini, Bill 'Foxy' Fowler, Brian Hutch and Tony Bramwell. Record producer Glyn Johns... managers and agents Deke Arlen and Harold Davison... publishers Terry & Mandy Oates... and of course, our dear photographer to the stars, the late and wonderful Harry Goodwin who even had an exhibition of his *TOTP* work at the Victoria & Albert Museum.

There were also the technical geniuses who made our work a doddle – vision mixer Richard 'Dicky' Pigg; camera crews 1 and 3 with their leaders, Ron Peverral and Ron Green. The extraordinary sound from Len Shorey, Dicky Green and Hugh Barker; the magical musical director Johnny Pearson and his flawless orchestra – visiting Americans were always confounded by how he was able to reproduce their charts! Gorgeous Samantha Juste, who lifted one's spirit every week just by being there... Richard Chamberlain, Cecil Korer and Colin Charman on the floor and above all, my dear friend and co-conspirator, Kate Greer, who I realised, when I came to America, was doing the work of about six people!

Then there were the amusing moments, when we started the show in an old church in Manchester, the singers had to lip sync to their recordings – P.J. Proby stretched his hands out to the audience and disappeared from view as he was pulled into the crowd, popping up every few seconds, still miming his song!

There's the 20 quid that Them (with singer Van Morrison) borrowed from me to get back to Ireland after their visit to the pub after the show, for which I am still waiting – 50 years later!

And always the fog in Manchester keeping musicians from arriving – as each band's turn came we had to resort to lighting only the lead singer, so you would have two Kinks, a Who and a Them masquerading as Herman's Hermits backing Peter Noone!

I learned an enormous amount from the 6 years I spent on *TOTP* about the art of television that has affected every show I have done since. Johnnie Stewart and I alternated producing and directing weekly, so we each did 26 shows a year, plus Christmas specials and recordings after each live show of acts (mostly visiting Americans) who we thought we would need in the future.

So over the years, I think I produced and directed about 156 *Top of the Pops* and loved every one of them and this 50th Anniversary *TOTP* book captures the very essence and spirit of those pioneering years of the programme.

Stanley Dorfman
August 2013

INTRODUCTION

Pan's People; hot pants; 'shaddap you face'; flares; hip hop; rap; Merseybeat; 'itsy-bitsy, teeny-weeny'; disco; grunge; Motown; Goth; dance; 'it's Chriiiiistmassss!'; mod; house; 'the fastest milkman in the west'; Britpop; Legs & Co; punk; drums & bass; Beckenham-based aliens; 'It's Number One! It's...'

Well, for a start, it's a programme which has been immortalised in song by the Kinks, Boomtown Rats, Mott the Hoople and, of course, the Rezillos (No.17, 1978, *Top of the Pops*).

However, this is not *just* the story of a long-running television programme. The history of *Top of the Pops* is also the story of British popular music; a shadow history of rock & roll, and beyond. It's the story of 'Auntie BBC' letting down her hair and getting down with the kids; and of how the initial 6-week run turned into a multi-generational, decades-long, pan-global TV phenomenon. Although nowadays, in this brave (if sometimes baffling) new world, where virtually every piece of recorded music is available at the press of a button, it is nigh on impossible to conjure up the strange and distant landscape in which *Top of the Pops* was first broadcast.

Imagine for a moment: a world without mobile phones or portable music and with a mere two black and white television channels; a nation in which over 75% of the electorate turn out to vote and where cigarettes are just 20p a packet. To the permanently switched-on young people of today, those distant days must seem as distant as the Cruikshank drawings that illustrated the weekly serials of Mr Charles Dickens.

But old-fashioned and clunky though those vintage *TOTP* may seem in retrospect, back in the day their potent mix of chart material, fashion and dancing proved an already integral part of a new, but fast-growing movement, that had yet to be christened 'pop culture'.

LEFT: *Disc spinner Samantha Juste (who later married the Monkees' Mickey Dolenz) with Pete Murray, one of the original* Top of the Pops *presenters, at a 1967 rehearsal*

Strangely, the timeless appeal of *Top of the Pops* was, if anything, helped rather than hindered by its strict guidelines. The programme's rules were laid down early on: only acts whose records were going *up* the charts were allowed on; no act was permitted to appear on two consecutive weeks – save for the nation's No.1; and every show ended with that all-important apex. At a time when the charts really mattered to pop fans and the pop business, that top slot was crucial to an artist's career.

For over 40 years, *Top of the Pops* remained an institution. Very soon after its 1964 launch its power became apparent, and thus, the brand became bigger than any individual band. The year of the programme's launch saw British pop music go global – and, within weeks of the first edition of *Top of the Pops* being broadcast, the Beatles made their first triumphant appearances in America, thereby opening the floodgates for the British Invasion and irrevocably altering the shape of our world.

During the programme's 1970s heyday, it was estimated that a quarter of the entire UK population tuned in to BBC1 on a Thursday evening to watch the latest acts strut their stuff. It could also be argued that the programme virtually created the Glam Rock craze. And even during the punk era of the late 1970s, the most anti-establishment acts seemed only too happy to do their snarling and sneering live on camera. When the acts themselves couldn't make it, *TOTP* became the shop window where you could enjoy their increasingly spectacular videos.

For several decades *Top of the Pops* became the mirror that nurtured and reflected every new musical style, fashion craze and youth movement. But as technology evolved to make the music more accessible, and as the record industry lost its stranglehold on that music, the programme's power inevitably diminished. It was clear that the writing was on the wall when its prime-time slot was altered; then its day of broadcast; then the channel… Until, in 2006, the BBC announced the unthinkable: it was removing *Top of the Pops* from its schedules entirely.

Shock! Horror! Outrage! – both from the record industry and the public at large. Yet ironically, with editions re-edited; episodes repeated; compilation CDs released and the growing interest in pop anniversaries… *Top of the Pops* proved, once again, to be bigger even than the music for which it provided a platform.

Strange to think that it all began in a former church in Manchester, at a time when 'pop music' was merely an insignificant trifle that kept young people amused. The last National Serviceman had been discharged just a few months before that historic first programme; the Beatles were strictly a UK phenomenon and Vietnam was still a faraway country of which we knew little.

Top of the Pops started out by offering the majority – who were strangers both to London and the Swinging 60s – a fascinating glimpse into a secret and exotic world. It went on to become the barometer of the British music industry, while helping to shape fashion and reflect changes in music and society. For every subsequent generation, it provided nothing less than the soundtrack to our lives.

Mick Jagger with original Top of the Pops *producer, Johnnie Stewart, backstage in 1969*

CHAPTER 1
The 1960s:
Skipping the Light Fandango

Forget the old cliché that if you can remember the 1960s you clearly weren't there. A far more accurate reflection is that the so-called Swinging 60s only really swung for about a couple of dozen people in London – most of them photographers, models, hairdressers or Cockney actors, plus, of course, a footballer, the Beatles and four of the Rolling Stones.

It was not until 1966 that *Time* magazine officially declared London to be 'swinging'. But by then, the image was already familiar: mini-skirted dolly birds swinging down Carnaby Street, while hip young men roared by in Minis accompanied by a blaring soundtrack of Fab music provided by the Who, Small Faces, Kinks, Dusty, Sandie and a hundred more. Pop music mirrored the times – at that time, more than any other.

But BBC radio was yet ready to hold up a mirror to prevailing fashion – in music or anything else. The familiar mid-60s soundtrack of non-stop-pop was instead provided by a motley collection of illegal pirate radio stations, bobbing queasily up and down on the North Sea – tantalisingly, just beyond the reach of British jurisprudence. Together, the two best known sea-faring stations – Radio Caroline and Radio London – provided a glittering soundtrack to that most illustrious of decades. Back then, ears pressed close to crackling transistor radios was how you heard the latest releases from the pantheon of pop greats.

It was not until 1967 that the government's Postmaster General (lest we forget, Labour politician Tony Benn) finally clamped down on the pirates, banning their broadcasts. And in September that year, the BBC reluctantly launched Radio 1.

Staid and behind the times BBC radio may have been. But just a few years earlier BBC television had definitely been ahead of the game when, on 1 January 1964, it broadcast the first ever episode of the UK's longest running television music programme.

The Beatles make their only live Top of the Pops *appearance on 16 June 1966, miming 'Paperback Writer'*

Despite all the naysayers who predicted a short shelf-life for rock & roll, there was a surprising number of precedents for pop on TV. In 1957, BBC Television (there was still only the one BBC channel) launched *Six-Five Special*. In 1958, ITV countered with *Oh Boy!* And in 1959, with sales of new-fangled 45 rpm singles overtaking those of 78s, BBC TV began the Saturday night institution that was *Juke Box Jury*. Commercial television hit back again: in 1961 with *Thank Your Lucky Star*s; and in 1963 – promising 'the weekend starts here' – with *Ready! Steady! Go!*

It was the BBC's Head of Variety, Bill Cotton (son of bandleader and Saturday night fixture Billy 'wakey, wakey' Cotton), who commissioned the corporation's counter-attack. Originally, *Top of the Pops* was only scheduled to run for six episodes, with the option of a further six should there be the demand.

Talking to Johnny Black in *Q* magazine in 1999, Cotton recalled: "At the time, *Ready! Steady! Go!* was doing amazing things... [a chart show] seemed simple and right, but there were, to say the least, trepidations within the organisation as to the potential of a show such as *Top of the Pops*. The feeling was, either it would be a total failure or a completely overwhelming success."

Later, talking to Jeff Simpson, Bill Cotton explained that the timing seemed just right for a new British pop programme: "What struck me was that the majority of the hit parade was British. Previously, it had been mostly American. But now, out of the Top 20, there were probably fifteen or sixteen British songs. Why didn't we do a hit parade show?"

The timing couldn't have been better. During the whole of 1963, both the LP and single charts in Britain were dominated by home-grown acts. Even prior to the Beatles' domination, Cliff Richard, the Shadows, Jet Harris & Tony Meehan, Frank Ifield – all had nailed the top slot down. And before you write in, Frank Ifield was born in Coventry, so definitely qualifies as a UK act! Then came the onslaught of the Beatles, and all the Liverpool groups who came in their wake. Gerry & the Pacemakers, the Searchers, Billy J. Kramer & the Dakotas... all enjoyed No.1 hit singles during that triumphant year of 1963. Only Elvis managed to muster a valiant rearguard action that year – but only for a single week when 'Devil In Disguise' was fleetingly at No.1.

Recognising that the time was right to celebrate the UK's dominance of the pop universe, the BBC gave *Top of the Pops* the go-ahead. Though as the corporation's house-magazine, *Radio Times*, solemnly announced:

"The performers whose songs are popular in the charts will mime to their discs, a departure from standard BBC policy. The idea is to replicate the sound of the popular track. No two performances are the same, but this performance is the one that made it a hit."

The BBC even had to negotiate a special dispensation with the all-powerful Musicians' Union to allow acts appearing on the show to mime to their own records. In order to protect the interests of their members, who were for the most part jobbing musicians, the Musicians' Union had always limited the amount of airplay permitted on the BBC. For years, the so-called needle-time restrictions had meant that only a limited number of discs could be played on the Corporation's pre-Radio 1, Light Programme; the remainder being replicated by BBC orchestras and singers. Elvis Costello's dad, Ross McManus, was among those who were kept busy throughout the 1960s, pretending to be any one of a hundred different chart stars.

"We feel it is dishonest for someone to just mouth the words," admitted one BBC executive at the time *Top of the Pops* launched. "We are relaxing the rules in this case because the programme is designed to let viewers hear records as recorded."

Johnnie Stewart – who had overseen previous TV pop programmes – *The Twist, The Trad Fad, Juke Box Jury* – was appointed as the show's first producer. Years later, discussing the durability of *TOTP*, Stewart reflected: "Those other shows at the time were kids' shows, for what is really a minority audience, and they had no peg to hang it on. We went for the charts – and there'll always be a pop chart."

Stewart continued as producer, steering the programme through its first 9 years before handing over to Robin Nash in 1973. But so identified with the programme had he become, that the image of the guy on the stool – seen on the show's end credits for years – was none other than... Johnnie Stewart!

Once the format was established, Johnnie Stewart stuck to two simple rules which the show continued to honour for much of its 42 year history: "It was so simple," Stewart told Steve Blacknell. "Rule Number One was that we only put a record in the show if it went up the charts that week. If a record was going down, to me it was dead. Rule Number Two: we always, and I mean *always*, ended with the No.1 record."

With the show finally green-lighted, there was a rush to gather together the necessary acts – as dictated by the most recent chart – and then to get them all up to the BBC studio in Manchester for that very first *Top of the Pops*.

Ironically, though 1964 was the high watermark of Beatlemania, the Fabs did not appear on that debut programme, despite having the No.1 single ('I Want To Hold Your Hand'); the No.3 single ('She Loves You'); two EPs (*The Beatles Hits*; *Twist & Shout*); *and* their second LP (*With The Beatle*s) – all in that week's Top 20 singles chart! There was sweet revenge though, as the first act featured on that very first edition of *Top of the Pops* was the Rolling Stones, performing 'I Wanna Be Your Man' – a song written by none other than Lennon & McCartney!

A further Fab irony occurred during the watershed week in March 1964 that saw the first-ever UK singles chart to feature nothing but UK acts – and the Beatles were absent from that show too! However, the Beatles did make their first appearance on the programme that same month, in a pre-recorded clip on which they mimed to their current single 'Can't Buy Me Love'.

* * *

The historic moment when the very first *Top of the Pops* episode was broadcast came at 6.35 p.m. on Wednesday 1 January 1964. And the first music was heard was the show's theme – 'Percussion Piece', written by Johnnie Stewart and Harry Rabinowitz and played by Bobby Midgley. Despite all the fluctuating pop fads and fashions, it would remain the *Pops*' theme until 1973.

Another enduring staple of the show was the voice announcing: "Yes... it's No.1... it's Top of the Pops!" This had been recorded one lunchtime by a BBC light entertainment radio producer called Jim Moir – who later went on to become the most influential figure in the UK pop industry when he became Controller of Radio 2.

Coincidentally, in 1963 while a young trainee at the BBC, Jim Moir had suggested to the corporation's Head of Light Entertainment, Tom Sloan, that the network should have a programme reflecting the seismic changes which the world of pop was undergoing during that Beatle-crazy year. But, as he remembered to Jeff Simpson, the Beeb were ahead of the game: "As I gave my brilliant exposition of this programme, Tom Sloan held his hand up and said 'Well Mr Moir, just in case you should ever think that we stole your idea, I should tell you that we in the Light Entertainment Group already have a similar show in mind'."

Dusty Springfield appears on the show in January 1964, promoting her debut solo single, 'I Only Want To Be With You'

When that very first show was broadcast, it was introduced by Jimmy Savile; the disc spinner was Denise Sampey; and there, live in the studio, miming to their latest hits were the Rolling Stones ('I Wanna Be Your Man'); Dusty Springfield ('I Only Want To Be With You'); the Dave Clark Five ('Glad All Over'); the Hollies ('Stay') and the Swinging Blue Jeans ('Hippy Hippy Shake'). On film, Cliff Richard and the Shadows performed 'Don't Talk To Him' and Freddie & the Dreamers did 'You Were Made For Me'. The studio audience got their brief moment in the spotlight when they were shown dancing, just a tad self-consciously, to the Beatles' 'She Loves You' and Gene Pitney's '24 Hours From Tulsa'.

And, that was it… a fantastic, fabulous, fluent snapshot of British pop music on the cusp of a new era. And only the late, great Gene Pitney flying the Stars & Stripes.

* * *

The reason the show came from Manchester was that, as today with its switch to Salford, the BBC wanted to maximise its use of regional studios, and their Manchester personnel weren't exactly over-extended. And as the power of the show became apparent, few managers showed any reluctance to dispatch their charges on that lengthy trek "up north". The journey took 5 hours and 15 minutes each way and cost £5. Though for an extra £1/6/- (£1.30p) each way, the biggest stars were sometimes treated to the luxury of a British Rail sleeper. With the ever-increasing influence of the programme, some managers even started stumping up £9/14/- for the air fare.

In time, as the power of *Pops* continued to build, flights would become the norm. As the Searchers' Frank Allen recalled: "In the very early days, of course, the show was produced at the old church in Dickenson Road, Manchester and those who were based in London would fly up from Heathrow early on the day, then catch the last plane down again after the show had finished – which was, as I recall, an 8.30 take-off.

"It was a pretty tight schedule but the airline was used to it and would be prepared for a bunch of pop stars checking in a bit late. The programme went out at 7 p.m., so there was naturally a mad dash by cab when it ended with the No.1 record at half-past. Just enough time to make the plane! The other Searchers were Liverpool-based but my home was in west London, so I was one of the mad dashers. Samantha Juste, who was the pretty girl who put the discs on the turntable every week, also had to collect her things and get to the waiting taxi every week. She was friendly and fun and we often used to share that final cab."

While that first show may have looked great on screen, the reality behind the camera was somewhat less than glamorous. Talking to Johnny Black the show's production secretary, Frances Line, remembered: "They'd taken all the pews out, but you could still clearly see that it was a church. It was very odd to see Camera One moving up and down what had very obviously been the aisle."

Things were not exactly cosy in the BBC Manchester canteen either. The Swinging Blue Jeans' Ray Ennis remembers an occasion when a dinner lady wanted to get autographs from some of the groups appearing on that first show,

Left: Jim Hendrix backstage at Top of the Pops *after performing 'Hey Joe', December 1966*

so one of his bandmates snatched a pen from another group on that historic show... "But Keith Richards demanded his pen back," Ennis told Johnny Black. "'You fuckin' Northern Ernies, give me my pen back!' So they started grappling over this little plastic pen... and they end up throwing punches on the floor. At this point, Mick Jagger comes in, sees what's going on, and wades in to help Keith, so it became a real free-for-all!"

Talking to Spencer Leigh, Ray Ennis remembered another mishap when the Blue Jeans were invited onto an early edition of the show to mime along to their big hit 'Hippy Hippy Shake', only to find their record being played at the wrong speed – which understandably affected their performance!

For the all-important first show, a studio audience had been rounded up from various Manchester youth clubs. They were not as fashionably dressed as their southern counterparts on *Ready! Steady! Go!*, but were clearly every bit as thrilled to be sharing a studio with their pop idols. For some acts too, the location was seen as a plus. Hollies' drummer Bobby Elliott was delighted that the first *TOTP* came from the group's hometown, but he also thought it worked better than its London equivalent: "Compared to *Ready! Steady! Go!* where you were always getting jostled by kids while you were trying to play, even the very first *Top of the Pops* was a model of organised perfection."

Not even the thorny question of miming bothered Elliott: "We didn't mind that because audio technology in those days couldn't capture a good live band sound for television. The sound on things like *Ready! Steady! Go!* which were live, was appalling! So on *Top of the Pops* you just took pride in how well you could match your movements to the record, which was quite a skill in itself.

"Our manager in London said 'Go up to Manchester, there's a new BBC show called *Top of the Pops*.' I remember saying at the time 'What a corny, un-hip name for a music show!'

"We were booked to perform our latest hit 'Stay', so off we went in our Ford Thames van, up the M1 – it ended just north of Watford Gap, and the rest of the journey was on the old A-roads. On arrival at Dickenson Road we found an old boarded-up church.

"Inside it had been converted into a TV studio. Quite cosy. Great little canteen with friendly ladies who served tea in proper cups on saucers...Doing the show was a doddle with dear old Johnnie Stewart directing. We just mimed and made it look real. Easy."

And so there it was: the historic first episode of a programme which was intended to run for six episodes – and went on for over two thousand!

Barely a month later, the blizzard which was the Beatles would go global when the Fabs conquered America. Their success paved the way for the British Invasion and, by the end of the year, what had been a largely UK phenomenon was reaching out across the Atlantic, as the Stones, Animals, Who, Yardbirds and Kinks took the music they loved back home.

As the only real rivals to the Beatles, the Rolling Stones made numerous appearances on the programme throughout the 1960s. Bill Wyman noted that the only Stones single not featured was 1964's 'Little Red Rooster' – though this was nothing to do with its bluesy authenticity, rather a run-in between the Stones' management and BBC mandarins.

As well as their run of timeless 60s hits ('Satisfaction', 'Get Off My Cloud', 'Paint It Black') the Stones were also allowed to feature odd album tracks on *Top of the Pops*: 'Mother's Little Helper' from 1966's *Aftermath*; a couple of songs from 1967's *Their Satanic Majesties Request*. The Stones were happy to play the promotional game, regularly appearing on *Pops*, but drawing the line at grinning inanely from the roundabout on *Sunday Night At The London Palladium*. Though, as Mick admitted: "The only reason we did the show was because it was a good national plug. Anyone who thought we were changing our image to suit a family audience was mistaken."

The band's reputation as bad boys persisted throughout the 60s – and following the famous Redlands drugs bust, the Stones released 'We Love You' – their answer song to the Beatles' 'All You Need Is Love'. With the very real threat of long-term prison sentences hanging over their heads, Mick Jagger and Keith Richards shot a film to promote their 1967 single. Based around the 19th Century trial of Oscar Wilde, it showed Mick preening himself as Oscar; Keith as a bespectacled judge; and Marianne Faithfull as the unbearably beautiful Bosie (Lord Alfred Douglas). Needless to say, it was deemed unsuitable for *TOTP*.

In July 1969, just days after Brian Jones' death and immediately prior to their first UK show in 2 years – which drew a crowd of half a million to London's Hyde Park – the Stones were due on the show to promote 'Honky Tonk Women'. The *TOTP* appearance "was not our greatest performance," Bill Wyman noted laconically.

Looking back at the band's *TOTP* appearances, it is hard to reconcile the boyish enthusiasm of Mick Jagger with the rock knight of today; the languorous cool of Keith Richards with the 21st Century's gnarled veteran... and poignantly, was there ever a more quintessential mid-60s pop star than Brian Jones?

"Greetings pop-pickers!" enthused Alan Freeman as he introduced the second *Top of the Pops*. A familiar voice on BBC radio since 1961, when he first hosted the Sunday night chart rundown on the old Light Programme, Freeman was seen as a safe pair of hands. And over the next three years he would remain one of the show's regular hosts, alongside Savile, Pete Murray and David Jacobs.

Freeman recalled: "My image was of happiness and joviality, because, after all, the music was lively and you had to be slightly over the top to give flow to the show." Only occasionally did Fluff's machine-gun patter falter, such as the time he introduced 'Cast Your Fate to the Wind' as – you guessed it – 'Cast Your Wind to the Fate'!

In November 1964, the *Radio Times* promised: "Alan Freeman introduces the guests, looks at today's chart, and speculates on trends in the world of Pop. The studio audience, as usual, take an active part in the proceedings." As with *Ready! Steady! Go!*, the audience was to become an integral part of the programme – looking back at them now, there is always the self-conscious, all-purpose dance step to accompany every act, and the quick guilty glance at the studio monitor to check whether they could be seen on TV at home.

David Jacobs had come to *TOTP* straight from years behind the desk smoothly controlling the panel on the Beeb's other longstanding pop show, *Juke Box Jury*. Jacobs hosted *Top of the Pops* equally effectively, running the show like an avuncular headmaster ("Even on the radio, he sounded as if he was wearing a suit and tie," Cilla Black told Ian Gittins).

Not much wonder that *Top of the Pops* made such a mark: *Juke Box Jury* was jaw-droppingly dull television, with absolutely no visual impact. Panelists were filmed *listening* to records! And then, for variety, audience members were shown – also listening to the records. The tension finally reached fever pitch when the panel voted the disc a 'Hit' or 'Miss'; then, occasionally, the star would emerge from behind a screen, smiling politely, to shake hands with the panel who had passed comment on their record.

RIGHT: *Official* TOTP *photographer Harry Goodwin snapping Peter Noone of Herman's Hermits*

Compare old episodes of *Juke Box Jury* with early *Top of the Pops* and spot the difference. Although the studio audiences were less excitable than those on later shows; the camera movements were more static than those later employed; and the sets were less exotic – there was already an energy and real vibrancy to the new kid on the TV block.

Our research revealed a fascinating internal BBC costing for one of the earliest editions of the programme. For presenting the 29 April 1964 edition of *Pops*, Alan Freeman received the princely sum of £105.00; while the comely, disc-spinning Samantha Juste got five guineas. There was also a surprisingly wide variation in payments to the musical performers, with the Merseybeats taking away £63.00; Gerry & the Pacemakers £157/10/-; Peter & Gordon £52/10/-; the Fourmost £63.00 while the Rolling Stones went home with £86.00! Photographer Harry Goodwin received £35.00; design ate up a whopping £182/2/3d while the all-important hospitality accounted for just six pounds and nine old pence! The *total* cost for that week's show was just £1,253/5/11d.

One man who knows all about this programme – and indeed most of our nation's TV history, is Dick Fiddy, who has been the British Film Institute's television consultant for the past quarter-century: "*Top of the Pops* arrived at a perfect time... Pop groups were replacing the old variety acts: you'd have a mixed variety bill, then gradually throughout the 60s, you'd work towards a mixed music bill. They would be mixed bills – the Beatles would have Frank Ifield on a bill, and *Top of the Pops* reflected that...

"It was the dog wagging the tail – the dog was the buying public, the tail was *Top of the Pops*, which reflected what the public was buying. It came at the right time, a very exciting time in music, when the BBC were finding their feet again after being heavily out-gunned by the early years of ITV. Under Sir Hugh Carlton-Greene in the early 60s, the Beeb put on *Steptoe & Son, That Was The Week That Was, Top of the Pops*, it began taking risks..."

Years later, when it became apparent that countless thousands of hours of priceless pop television had been wiped by the BBC so that the tapes could be re-used, there was a general sense of outrage. But then hindsight is a wonderful thing, as Dick Fiddy confirmed: "Pop music – more than most television – was considered ephemeral, so the reason for not keeping it was doubly so. I mean *nobody* had any idea that these groups, those songs, would have a 50-year shelf-life. Nobody!

"It's very easy to point the finger and talk about cultural vandalism, and the loss of these programmes – but, at the time, you were hard pushed to see what the BBC could have done... You can use the tapes again, so there was a financial imperative. The BBC has always had an uneasy relationship with newspapers, and if the *Daily Mail* or *Daily Express* had found that the BBC was sitting on thousands of tapes which they could have re-used, which they can't show again because they're out of copyright, then they would have pilloried them for the waste of license payers' money! Financially, they did the right thing; culturally, as we now know, it's shocking."

Those first *Top of the Pops* editions from Manchester were genuine seat-of-the-pants television. The entire programme was broadcast live; the producers only received the final chart on Tuesday morning; and within 36 hours Johnnie Stewart and the team had to have a complete show ready to broadcast live on air! It was, as Stewart would later ruefully admit: "the simplest show in the world – and pure murder to put on!"

The Kinks made their *TOTP* debut with 'You Really Got Me' on 19 August 1964 – just a fortnight after its release as a single. Equally significant is the fact that the journey from London to Manchester to record the show was the band's first-ever flight! Over the next couple of years the Kinks became regulars on the show, as their list of classic 60s singles: 'Tired Of Waiting', 'Dedicated Follower Of Fashion', 'Sunny Afternoon', 'Waterloo Sunset', so beautifully reflected those fast-changing times.

Many groups have been lauded as defining that decade, and thanks to periodic use on TV documentaries, feature films and DVDs, certain songs have become entrenched in the public consciousness. But no other group has ever made the same impact, or maintained such an influence, as the Beatles. Incredible then, given their dominance of the UK pop scene during the 7 years they spent at the top, that it was not until June 1966 that the Beatles made their first and only live appearance on *Top of the Pops*.

It was between recording sessions for *Revolver* that the group consented to appear. According to a breathless report in that week's *New Musical Express*, Brian Epstein said: "Johnnie Stewart wrote me a letter saying that although he had scheduled a Beatles film-clip for the programme, there had been an unprecedented demand for them to appear live on the show... I put it to the boys late on Tuesday and they said 'yes'."

'The boys' historic debut took place in Studio 2 at the BBC's Television Centre in Shepherd's Bush on Thursday 16 June 1966. The group spent nearly 6 hours rehearsing, posing for photos and further camera rehearsals – and then, live on air, the Beatles played live, albeit miming, to their current single 'Paperback Writer' and its B-side 'Rain'.

Mark Lewisohn, the world's foremost Beatle authority, has observed of that historic June 1966 appearance: "Ironically, it was not just the group's first personal appearance on the show, nor just their first before any TV audience in 10 months, it was also (excepting the unique worldwide transmission of 'All You Need Is Love' on 25 June 1967) their last live musical television appearance of all, and certainly their last on a recognised 'pop show'. Johnnie Stewart could never have played a better winning hand."

Prior to this ground-breaking appearance (and indeed, subsequently), the group had produced little film clips with which to promote their current single – which, as the songs inevitably wound their way to the "toppermost of the poppermost", the programme would screen. Sometimes, however, *TOTP* would concoct their own little clip to run while the song was playing. Mark Lewisohn, for example, noted that for the double A-sided 'Yellow Submarine'/ 'Eleanor Rigby', the programme filmed: "Eleven members of the British Sub Aqua Club in action at a London swimming pool, while for the latter, stringing together a sequence of stills of a BBC scene-shifter (who also happened to be a former actor) dressed as a priest and posing with props in a Manchester cemetery." Another memorable *TOTP* sequence accompanied 'Ticket To Ride' – not a Fab in sight, just that speeded-up London to Brighton train ride which was so familiar to black and white TV audiences of the 1960s.

Inevitably though, as the Beatles' music grew more elaborate, so did their videos. From straightforward mimed performances, Beatle clips evolved through the worldwide anthem of 1967 'All You Need Is Love' (actually shot for the BBC's *Our World* programme), while the promos for 'Penny Lane' and 'Strawberry Fields Forever' perfectly captured the hazy mood of the times.

One intriguing *Top of the Pops* clip that survives from the 1960s has Alan Freeman tantalisingly introducing a 1967 round-up in the Christmas schedule,

LEFT: *A bird's eye view of the Rolling Stones performing on the show in 1965*

and alerting viewers that the Fabs' *Magical Mystery Tour* will be screened later that night on BBC1 which, he knowingly informs us, is "not one to miss".

Of course, the one star who never made it to Manchester, London, or indeed any edition of *Top of the Pops*, was the undisputed King of Rock & Roll... Elvis Presley. At the time when his thunder was increasingly being stolen by the young beat groups of the 60s, Elvis was still only in his 30s; but, increasingly locked into the Hollywood treadmill for most of the 1960s, Elvis remained the King across the water. The only time Elvis ever set foot in any part of the UK was in 1960 returning from Army service in Germany, when his plane stopped to refuel at Prestwick in Scotland. Legend has it that he spent half an hour chatting to fans and had a cup of tea!

Although 60s bands like the Beatles, Stones and Who may have eclipsed him, the King still enjoyed a substantial run of UK chart singles during the decade. And when Elvis's single 'Crying in the Chapel' gave him a surprise No.1 in 1965, the ever-imaginative Johnnie Stewart snatched some photos of a Manchester church and intercut them with photos of Elvis.

But when it came to *Top of the Pops* and photographs, there was really only one man – Mancunian Harry Goodwin. Approached early on by Johnnie Stewart to become the programme's official photographer, Harry was flattered, though less than delighted to learn that his weekly fee would be a mere £30. Even Mick Jagger thought that was a bit low, and advised Harry to demand more. To pour oil on troubled financial waters, Stewart offered to give Harry his own end credit: 'Still Photographer: Harry Goodwin'. It was a position Harry maintained until 1973.

The Small Faces was another of those now legendary 60s acts who were regular guests on the programme. Drummer Kenney Jones had nothing but fond memories of the band's appearances: "It seemed to be one big happy family. In the mid-60s of course there'd be a much greater cross-section of artists appearing on the show; some weeks you'd be performing alongside people like Val Doonican and Ken Dodd, but they were always really concerned about you, very polite, and into your career. No problems whatsoever."

Small Faces' singer Steve Marriott was somewhat less enchanted, and went so far as to insult the powerful, and generally admired, producer Johnnie Stewart to his face. Legend has the pugnacious singer confronting Stewart with the words: "I'm glad you're leaving, I always thought you were a major c**t." Alas, Marriott was misinformed, and Stewart was staying put... Instead, it was the Small Faces who "left" – becoming the first band to be actually banned from the programme.

A breakdown of the accounts for the 1 April 1965 edition reveals that Samantha Juste's pay has doubled to a full *ten* guineas, while Jimmy Savile gets a whole £41.00 more than poor old Fluff. Among the acts, Them (featuring Van Morrison) are paid £52/10/-; Cliff Richard £78/15/-; Unit 4+2, the Animals and the Yardbirds all make do with £63.00; and the Who get £76/13/-. Perhaps rather recklessly, given Keith Moon's proclivities, 15 guineas is lavished on the hire of *two* drum kits!

Unit 4+2's Lem Lubin laughed as he looked back to those days when a trip to Manchester was essential, even after they hit the top with 'Concrete & Clay': "Back at the start it only took us 2 hours to drive up to Manchester – well there were no speed limits and we were in a hurry! If we did stop on the way up or on our return, it was protocol for all the bands to stop at the legendary Blue Boar Inn. It was there that us, the Who, the Kinks, the Stones.... well, *everyone* would stop for a break. Oh, and steal sandwiches (it was mandatory!).

"It's weird, but when 'Concrete & Clay' hit No.1, it didn't really hit *us*. Dear Kenny Everett and Dave Cash had really made that record for us on the pirate Radio London, bless 'em... Maybe it was too big to take in, but it was kind of like 'Oh okay, that's great; let's have another round of drinks!' If we ever *did* realise we had made it, well, it was when the BBC put us up in a hotel in Altrincham to do the show. It cost £4.00 a night! We couldn't believe it – a real hotel! If nothing else, *Top of the Pops* made us feel just a bit important; and that maybe – just *maybe* – we were part of the bigger picture!"

Cliff Richard (now, *Sir* Cliff) had already been enjoying hit records for 6 years by the time the first edition aired. With an incredible and unparalleled career, Sir Cliff is in the unique position of having enjoyed hit records for every decade the UK charts have been in existence. And equally remarkable is the fact that throughout the entire history of *Top of the Pops*, Sir Cliff has racked up more appearances than any other act – an estimated 160 throughout the history of the show.

The 1965 Christmas Day edition of the show serves as a potent reminder of just who was flying high in the pop firmament at that crucial moment in pop history: the Beatles were amply represented on film, but live performances were featured from the Rolling Stones, Georgie Fame, the Kinks, Moody Blues, the

Walker Brothers, the Seekers... and Ken Dodd.

It is worth remembering just how popular the buck-toothed balladeer still was at that midway point of the Swinging 60s. Nineteen sixty-five was a year that saw keynote releases from the Beatles, Beach Boys, the Who, Simon & Garfunkel, the Byrds, Them and Bob Dylan – but, despite all this hip competition, Ken Dodd's 'Tears' remained the UK's No.1 single for 5 weeks.

In total, Dodd's single spent nearly 6 *months* on the charts; and on the back of its durability, *TOTP*'s rival, ITV's *Thank Your Lucky Stars*, actively discouraged appearances by "long-haired groups". Instead, they promoted "good music" – and the first act they chose was none other than... Ken Dodd! And as final testament to Dodd's musical powers – even in that hippest of all decades, let it be remembered that second-only to singles by the Beatles, Ken Dodd's 'Tears' was – incredibly – the biggest-selling single of the entire 1960s.

Such astonishing diversity may have helped account for the programme's enduring ability, but it also increased the frustration felt by many at having to sit through balladeers and comedians, before getting to see their cutting-edge favourites. Thanks to repeats, you can relish again the soft folk of the Seekers, bolstered by the unparalleled and undervalued voice of Judith Durham. Or look again at the unequal pairing of Sonny & Cher, then look at the audience looking at the odd couple, and, finally, wonder if you will *ever* again be able to hear 'I Got You Babe' without thinking of the film *Groundhog Day*. There is an added poignancy in watching those old re-runs of the few shows that survive from the 60s: just realising how few of the Byrds, the Dave Clark 5, and the Beatles remain...

It was early in 1966 that the programme finally made the inevitable move South, from Manchester to the BBC's Lime Grove studios in London – where the new space gave Stewart much more flexibility in presenting the acts. That same year saw a further fundamental change in the way *Top of the Pops* was made. Until 1966 the Musicians' Union had been happy enough to have acts miming along to their own records. But now there was a growing concern that their members were being done out of work, which led to the introduction of a complicated new system. The acts themselves were still welcome on the show, but they had to get there earlier in order to pre-record their hit. That was fine for a four-piece group who played their own instruments. But as pop grew increasingly complex during 1966, and particularly in the following psychedelic year of '67, it meant that if in addition to the artist or band there was a full orchestra and backing singers on the disc… then *that* line-up is what had to be replicated when they performed on *Top of the Pops*.

The first *Top of the Pops* broadcast from London, on 20 January 1966, was hosted by David Jacobs, who introduced studio guests Cilla Black ('Love's Just A Broken Heart'); Otis Redding ('My Girl'); Paul & Barry Ryan ('Have Pity on the Boy'); David & Jonathan ('Michelle'); Crispian St Peters ('You Were On My Mind'); Herman's Hermits ('A Must To Avoid'); Stevie Wonder ('Uptight'); Herb Alpert ('Spanish Flea', on film); and that week's No.1, the Spencer Davis Group with 'Keep On Running'.

Moving to London allowed for larger studios and more lavish sets. That meant bigger audiences, which could of course, now be drawn from the trendy, and by then world-famous, streets of 'Swinging London'.

Even when the show had come from the less-trendy north, the audience had always been as integral a part of *Top of the Pops* as the acts who appeared on the show. And of course, what the acts and audience were wearing was every bit as important as what the audience was listening to. Though in hindsight, it is often forgotten that those early editions of *Top of the Pops* were broadcast in black and white, so in a sense, the viewers had to imagine for themselves the bright colours and vibrant fashions.

But by the time *Top of the Pops* came south, London was already recognised as the cynosure of all things "happening". Besides being home to the Beatles and all the leading pop groups of the period, film stars like Terence Stamp, Sarah Miles, Michael Caine, Julie Christie, Tom Courtenay and Susannah York were now icons across the world. Even the hairdresser Vidal Sassoon had become a celebrity. And in fiction, it was London from which James Bond, 007, ventured out on his glamorous missions. Photographers too were now in on the game – with the likes of David Bailey, Terence Donovan and Brian Duffy bringing freshness and excitement to the moribund fashion industry. Their success was confirmed when cinema maestro Michelangelo Antonioni came to the capital to film his take on 'Swinging London', *Blow-Up* – whose protagonist was a fashion photographer.

But whoever was wearing what, it soon became apparent that particularly during its 60s heyday, *Top of the Pops* exerted a strong visual hold over its television audience. The mini skirt soon gave way to the *Bonnie & Clyde* midi and *Dr Zhivago* maxi… outlandish hippie gear was replaced by the more rural cottons. On into the 70s, denim and glam, skinhead belt and braces and ripped punk jeans… whatever the style, you like as not saw it first on *Top of the Pops*.

During the 1960s, Chris Welch of *Melody Maker* was a regular visitor to the *Top of the Pops* studio in London. "Looking back, it was amazing," Chris told us. "I just drove up to Television Centre in my Ford Consul, was waved in, and parked right outside. Imagine that today! The first time I went was in 1965, just trotted up to reception – '*Melody Maker* to see Tom Jones on *Top of the Pops*' – and they waved you through without looking up from their copy of *Titbits*!

"But the actual studios were a bit of a disappointment. On television, even in black and white, it all looked so glamorous and exciting, but when you got there the studio was rather gloomy and tatty looking; very dark, all those long dark corridors, and a Dalek looking like it was standing guard outside the *Top of the Pops* studio.

"The managers and PRs always liked sending journalists to do interviews with their artist at *Top of the Pops* – whether it was Tom Jones or Jimi Hendrix or the Small Faces… It was almost to remind you as a journalist that their act had made it."

Chris's opposite number on the rival paper *New Musical Express* was Keith Altham, who had similar memories: "You could always guarantee nailing two or three interviews if you went up to the studio during rehearsals. We had some great times. After the show had moved to White City, we were in the bar there, and Ray Davies who'd had a few, was having a go at Dave Hill, trying to prove he was wearing a wig! He launched at him and Chas Chandler had to step in to rescue the situation!

"Dusty had three wigs – Sandie, Lulu and Cilla! One time I was with her in her dressing room at the *Pops* and she said 'Do you like football?' Which I did – and so for the next half hour we kicked her wigs around the room! Dusty was many things but she was never *ever* boring!

"Another time when I was in Dusty's dressing room doing an interview with her, a knock came on the door and a face popped into view: 'Would you mind keeping the noise down?' a mop-haired lad enquired. 'We're trying to rehearse next door.' Dusty, who had a bit of a temper, said a few unkind words and threw an ashtray at him. The door slammed shut – and that was how Brian Jones avoided having his block knocked off!"

RIGHT: 'Little' Stevie Wonder in 1965 - one of the earliest UK visits by a Tamla-Motown act

* * *

One thing that never changed on *Top of the Pops* was the audience. Of course, the audience-members changed over the years; what they wore changed; and what they listened to *definitely* changed. But down the years, the crowd always clustered round the artist who is performing, staring wide-eyed or lustfully at their idol – who is *so* tantalisingly close, yet *so* far away. And watch them trying to watch themselves: every episode will have at least one teenager tearing their eyes away from the act in order to try and catch sight of themselves on the studio monitor. In the days before home video recording, YouTube or iPlayer, just one glimpse could ensure a fleeting taste of pop star status.

But, according to Chris Welch, the *TOTP* audience could be quite a dangerous place to be: "Those huge old cameras on dolleys went crashing across the studio to get a shot of the singer, and they weren't too concerned about anyone getting in their way, so if you were on the studio floor, you quite often found yourself prodded and pushed, it was like a rugby scrum at times."

Lon Goddard, then writing for *Record Mirror*, has similar memories of his visits to the BBC studios: "The motorized crane cameras wheeled around the slick, shiny floor of the *Top of the Pops* studio like the famous teacup spin-around ride at Disneyland. While taping the artist from every direction, it was quite remarkable the way they swooped around cutting a swathe through the walls of gyrating girls like giant Daleks on speed."

Despite the instrumental virtuosity and musical progress being made in pop music during that frenziedly inventive period, one thing remained stubbornly the same.... The acts were still expected to come on to the programme, and then stand there mouthing along to their hits! One of the best-remembered *Top of the Pops* moments from the 1960s illustrated the crazy situation around miming. Long hailed as rock's most inventive guitarist, Jimi Hendrix was waiting to perform 'Purple Haze', when the backing track started booming out the Alan Price Set's hit 'Simon Smith And His Amazing Dancing Bear'. Caught unawares, Jimi laughed... "I like the voice, man, but I don't know the words!"

One of the real surprise hits during 1967, coming against the Beatles, Procol Harum and other Summer of Love favourites, was 'Seven Drunken Nights' by the Dubliners. Part of its success was due to a black and white promo film, shot by Peter Whitehead. Talking to Neil Spencer in 2012 about the making of the film, the director recalled a pub crawl with the group around Dublin, and later waking up "in bed with a beautiful red-headed girl and nothing else – no money, no camera and no memory!" Fortunately for him, his assistant had rescued the 60 minute film, "of which 50 minutes were totally and absolutely unusable". Luckily though, there were just enough shots of a horse and cart, and numerous pints of Guinness, that, skillfully edited, could be shown on *TOTP* that week – alongside Jeff Beck and the Who – thus launching the Dubliners' career.

Of the triptych of songs that hallmarked that Summer Of Love ('San Francisco', 'All You Need Is Love'), perhaps *the* defining sound was Procol Harum's other-worldly 'A Whiter Shade Of Pale'. It remained at the top of the UK charts for 6 weeks, thereby earning the band a run of *Pops* appearances that year. A surviving clip shows vocalist Gary Brooker dressed up like Fu Manchu as the studio audience waltzed to the song. In the rush to be everywhere that summer, Procol Harum shot a promo film for their anthem. Directed by Peter Clifton (who later went on to helm the Led Zeppelin concert film *The Song Remains the Same*) it showed the band looking suitably moody and mysterious as they prowled the grounds of Worcestershire's Witley Court. To add some grit and topical relevance, newsreel shots of the war raging in Vietnam were inter-cut, leading *Top of the Pops* producer Johnnie Stewart to ban the clip. As he told *Disc & Music Echo*: "I don't want war pictures like that on my show!"

But for all the 'peace & love' in the air during 1967, Gary Brooker recalled it was not always thus: "We appeared several times when 'A Whiter Shade of Pale' was No.1, each time with me singing live to the original backing track. On one of these occasions Engelbert Humperdinck was also on... I remember feeling very peeved that his 'Release Me' had kept the Beatles' 'Strawberry Fields' and 'Penny Lane' from the No.1 slot. Now he had his next hit, 'There Goes My Everything' roaring up the charts, but what he hadn't reckoned with was Procol getting in the way – totally from off the wall.

"I bravely approached Engel, who was quite a big bloke, and said 'There, that'll teach you to mess with the Beatles!' He made no reply but he was smoking a big cigar at the time, and blew a huge mouthful into my face. It was grounds for a fight but, as I said, he was a big bloke and this was after all the hallowed grounds of the BBC, and it was the Summer of Love, and we were all meant to love each other…"

Yet looking back, "Engel" was not the only less-than-hip artist charting in 1967.

A *Pops* from March that year, hosted by the 42-year-old – and by his own admission avuncular – Pete Murray, introduced performances from Frank & Nancy Sinatra; Cliff Richard; the Supremes; Engelbert Humperdinck; and Dave Dee, Dozy, Beaky, Mick & Tich. Aside from Jimi Hendrix, there was little here for readers of *International Times*.

And talking about moody and mysterious bands… Legendary now as the band who took their music to the very edge of known space, it seems hard to credit that back at the beginning of their career, Pink Floyd were as happy as any other act to appear on *Top of the Pops*.

Nevertheless, the Floyd's label, EMI, were still concerned about the band attracting the wrong audience – going so far as to issue the following statement in 1967: "Not knowing what people mean by 'psychedelic pop', the Pink Floyd refuse to use the phrase about their stage presentation. They are not seeking to create hallucinatory effects on their audiences, their only idea is to entertain." A recently discovered clip of the Floyd on the show has them in all resplendent in their psychedelic glory – although, of course, just like everyone else – in black and white…

By the summer of 1967 the Floyd had two singles out, and their second, 'See Emily Play', earned them the first of three appearances on the *Top of the Pops*. Chris Welch of *Melody Maker* remembers bumping into the Floyd's legendary leader Syd Barrett backstage, who mused: "It's beautiful here. I never go anywhere else. You meet interesting people prepared to like me. That's very nice."

Unfortunately though, by the time of Pink Floyd's final appearance, on 27 July 1967, things in Syd's happy world had gone awry, marking the onset of a decline from which he would never return. "By the third week," Floyd expert Glenn Povey later wrote, "he was disheveled, unshaven and in rags, with a careless attitude, uninterested in performing, and insisting that if John Lennon didn't have to appear on the show, then neither did he!"

Following *Top of the Pops*' move to the BBC's Lime Grove studios, the show also gained some fresh new hosts. Hot from the newly-launched BBC Radio 1, came Stuart Henry, Emperor Rosko, Kenny Everett, Dave Cash and Simon Dee.

To his credit, David Jacobs saw the psychedelic writing on the wall, and gave up presenting the programme in 1967 after four years. "The audience in the studio were getting so much younger," he explained to Ian Gittins. "I was in the wrong place. I had a lovely time, but I just felt that I was too old and too square."

Stanley Dorfman and Roy Orbison on the Derry & Toms roof garden in London, making a promotional film of Oh Pretty Woman *for TOTP transmission*

Pete Murray, who remained on the programme for almost 6 years, spoke to Shaun Tilley about Jacobs' departure: "David never really felt comfortable on the programme. Alma Cogan said 'David Jacobs is a sitting down compere rather than a standing up one!' His replacement, Simon Dee, was quite difficult, he was quite opinionated and never really fitted in... When I was doing the show I never wore anything casual, I always went on wearing a suit, looking like a bank manager, and I did that because I wanted to be different – I've never worn a pair of jeans in my life!"

Despite the patchouli-tinged belief that in 1967 everyone went round wafting incense and jangling their bells, there is an intriguing clip from the period in which Malcolm Muggeridge interviews the BBC's first Director General, Lord Reith. The conservative Muggeridge is clearly appalled by the notion that untold millions could be watching the same programme at the same time on their infernal television sets. As the man who began it all, Reith agrees, shaking a dour head and agreeing that television was a "potential social menace of the first magnitude". Sadly, Reith's views on *TOTP* go unrecorded.

Looking back, it is hard to appreciate just how quickly fame could arrive in the pop music firmament of the 1960s. I remember interviewing Maurice Gibb who said it was still hard to believe that one day "we were reading about the Beatles in Australia, then 6 weeks later I was sitting in a nightclub in London chatting to John Lennon!"

Billed as "the new Beatles" on the back of their striking UK single debut 'New York Mining Disaster 1941', the Bee Gees made their first British TV appearance on *Top of the Pops* on 11 May 1967. Maurice recalled sharing the programme with Lulu, the Move and the Rolling Stones. Speaking to Jeff Simpson, Lulu later recalled that fateful meeting: "I'd heard that one of the little Bee Gees fancied me... I wondered 'Which one?' because I thought they were all cute. And of course I met up with them at *Top of the Pops* and that was the beginning of my romance, which subsequently ended up in marriage to Maurice Gibb!"

Neil Innes recalls that when the Bonzo Dog Band were asked on the show for the fourth time to promote their 1968 'Urban Spaceman' hit, drummer 'Legs' Larry Smith suggested the band treat it like an episode of *Come Dancing*. Subsequently, half the Bonzos appeared in ball gowns, the other half in tuxedos with numbers on their backs, but perplexingly, no trousers!

But not everyone was impressed... Marmalade, who were No.1 that week with 'Ob La Di, Ob La Da', had vowed to appear in full Scottish regalia were they lucky enough to hit the top spot. And "sure enough," Neil remembered, "just when we were all dressed up, they knocked on our door to show us their kilts. Their disappointment was unconcealed."

Marmalade's drummer Alan Whitehead also remembered the occasion: "As a mainly Scottish band we had always said that if we ever got to No.1, we would wear kilts on the show. So, when 'Ob La Di, Ob La Da' did it in the January of 1969 it was most definitely on the cards. I was actually the only non-Scot in the band, so I got dressed as a Grenadier Guard while they were all kilted up! We were sharing a dressing room with the Bonzo Dog Band, and they – true to form – were dressed half man and half woman! You could only imagine the face on the concierge as he popped his head round the door ...!

"We did a 5 p.m. dress rehearsal – with the lads in their kilts with *nothing* on underneath, and when it was time for the final run through they decided it was 'Can Can' time! To much consternation we later went live with the boys with yellow stickers over their wedding tackle and shot from the waist up only!

"I was not that easily star-struck, but one time I went off for a pee, and there – resplendent with the deepest dyed hair I had *ever* seen – taking a leak was... Roy Orbison! The rumours were always that he was, in fact, an albino, but to be honest, who cared, he was a *legend*. All I could think to say was 'Good evening, Mr Orbison'. To which he replied: 'Good evening son,' and just left me... Gobsmacked!"

Love Affair were still incredibly young when they broke big, as singer Steve Ellis recalled: "The first *Top of the Pops* I did was with Love Affair, when I was 17. 'Everlasting Love' had gone in at No.36 – we were on cloud nine. Our drummer was only 15, and we were prone to playing all sorts of pranks on each other. With a mixture of nervousness and teenage kicks, we removed the nut and bolt from his drum stool and replaced them with some matchsticks! The show was live then... Anyway, Love Affair were announced, the said matchsticks snapped as he sat on the stool and said drummer collapsed in a heap on the floor, live on TV – job done! Luckily, Johnnie Stewart, the producer, saw the funny side of it. Just as well, as we did *Top of the Pops* for five consecutive weeks thereafter – with 'Everlasting Love' finally climbing to the coveted No.1 with half a million sales.

"Manfred Mann were on with us one week when they were No.1. with 'Mighty Quinn'. Mike D'Abo (a good pal now) had a rather large bulge in the front of his trousers, which was the cause of much whispered discussion. Anyway, Johnnie Stewart walked into the studio, fixed Mike with a steely look and said 'Mr D'Abo, would you kindly remove that toilet roll from the front of your trousers, *Top of the Pops* is a family show!' Mike retreated backstage and came back out rather less bulky in the trouser department. Of course being a bunch of teenage kids we found this hysterical, but poor Mike was rather crestfallen."

Another of those key 60s bands, the Who made their first *Top of the Pops* appearance early in 1965, when their debut single 'I Can't Explain' was picked as a 'Tip for the Top'. The West London Mods dutifully made their way to the Manchester studios to mime along, and the single eventually reached No.8. A later appearance on a *Top of the Pops* New Year's Eve special, when Keith Moon was at the height of his 'Moon the Loon' phase, saw the drummer playing a transparent drum kit, with Viv Stanshall placed behind him operating a rope attached to his wrist whenever the camera alighted on him.

Even Pete Townshend's famous windmill style of guitar playing was all due to *Top of the Pops*: "In those days it was sent out live..." he told Dave Marsh, "and we had to mime our record, thus, it was a cinch. No worries about throats, or atmosphere, or getting in tune... just what colour pants to wear or what silly outfit to put on to get the camera's attention. Keith would get about 80% of the camera time... [so] every time the camera swung to me, I would swing my arm like a maniac!"

In 1966, nearly a decade before 'Bohemian Rhapsody', the Who had a short film screened on *Top of the Pops* to promote 'Happy Jack'. Filmed in black and white, it was directed by Michael Lindsey-Hogg (who later directed the Beatles' *Let It Be*) and shot in the style of a Keystone Cops comedy.

The constant demand for personal appearances by the big acts of the era meant that those little filmed promo films – precursors of the pop video – became invaluable. Keith Richards told Jeff Simpson: "You'd be in Australia and you've got a new record out in the UK, so you'd say: 'Is it all right if we send you a film clip?'"

Given the "flying by the seat of our pants" tension that preceded *Top of the Pops* every week, the producers came more and more to rely on their own films. Who can forget Roy Orbison strolling around Derry & Toms' roof garden miming 'Oh Pretty Woman'... Though some were less successful: what, for goodness sake, had ducks on a pond to do with Bob Dylan's 1969 hit 'Lay Lady Lay'?

An invitation to appear on *Top of the Pops* was always welcome – offering proof positive that you had "arrived". But the thorny issue of miming still rankled with many acts, particularly those who prided themselves on their authenticity and core musical values. Van Morrison, for one, was quoted in Johnny Rogan's exhaustive biography grumbling about his band's betrayal of their roots: "Them were never meant to be on *Top of the Pops*. I mean, miming? Lip synching? We used to laugh at that programme, think it was a joke."

Legend has it that when Pentangle appeared on *Top of the Pops* in 1969, performing 'Light Flight' – their theme from the BBC1 drama *Take Three Girls*, guitar legend Bert Jansch not only didn't mime, but actually fell asleep during the performance. Asked by Pete Paphides to clarify this, Bert explained in those quiet, clipped Caledonian tones: "With the exception of Jacqui [McShee, Pentangle's singer], we were all miming, [so] I had nothing to do!"

On that thorny question of miming, a word here about the girl whose job it was to spin the discs, thus emphasising that all the acts who appeared on the show *were* miming. The first girl – and it was *always* a girl – was production assistant Denise Sampey. But she was soon replaced by "dolly bird" Samantha Juste, who remains the programme's best-remembered disc spinner. Seated beside the DJ console, she smiled sweetly, and delicately placed a 45 on the old Dansette just before the cameras cut to the group standing nearby and mouthing the words along with that record. Of course, this was all for show; the music that was actually heard being provided by a BBC tape operator in the gallery.

Manchester-born Samantha had been a model before starting work behind the scenes on *Top of the Pops*. After being promoted to the other side of the camera, she spun winsomely alongside the first four presenters, garnering a fee of 10 guineas (£10.50) for each appearance. But perhaps her real legacy from the job was the fact that Samantha caught the eye of pop idol Mickey Dolenz of the Monkees. They became quite the couple, and were married in 1968.

On arriving in the UK in 1967, visiting American Tony Visconti (soon to produce David Bowie and Marc Bolan) was frankly baffled by *Top of the Pops*: "I was perplexed by the variety of music on the weekly chart show," he recounted in his autobiography. "When I arrived in London I had no idea that the British public could have such bad taste, while simultaneously nurturing the greatest rock stars in history…"

As if to compound Visconti's bafflement, the 200th edition of *TOTP* in November 1967 featured the Kinks; Dave Dee, Dozy, Beaky, Mick & Tich; the Foundations; the Who; Dave Clark 5; Donovan and... Val Doonican. Also Gene Pitney, valiantly miming along to 'Something's Gotten Hold Of My Heart', but fluffing the words and instead mouthing "whatever came into my head...". Studio guests who dropped by included 40% of the Bee Gees, Lulu, Paul Jones, Alan Price, Graham Nash of the Hollies, and the man who was born to be a recluse, Scott Walker.

By the time of its bicentenary, *Top of the Pops* had seen off all manner of TV competition. *Ready! Steady! Go!* had come off air in late 1966, as had other programmes aimed specifically at the burgeoning youth audience, such as *A Whole Scene Going* and *Gadzooks! It's All Happening*. But although it had only been on air for a couple of years, by 1966 *Melody Maker*'s Chris Welch was already asking "What's wrong with television pop?"

Before quoting producers and directors, Welch fulminated: "It's a question that has been asked since the early days of *Cool For Cats*... But recently, the clamour of criticism has reached spectacular heights – from the public, in newspapers, magazines and on television. Critical emphasis has shifted from the all-out *Expresso Bongo* type of frontal attack on Pop to selective sniping at TV shows like... *Top of the Pops*... which [is] slammed as pretentious, repetitive, usually uninteresting, or worse... The real source of irritation is that the same shows are presenting the same artists in the same way, week after week."

❊ ❊ ❊

Four years after the show's debut, the original *TOTP* dance troupe, the Go-Jos, were replaced by Pan's People, who made their debut dancing to Tommy James & the Shondells' 'Mony Mony'. Aside from the visual appeal of the scantily-clad dancers, Pan's People were another useful weapon in the *TOTP* arsenal – if a particular act was not available, instead of the customary 'mini film' choreographer Flick Colby could work up a routine for her girls.

After arriving in London from New York, Flick met the core of her dance troupe at a studio in 1966; wisely rejecting the name Dionysius Darlings, they instead deferred to the God of Dance, and Pan's People became a core element of the *Pops*. Sometimes the troupe had just a few hours to rehearse a routine, and then there was the all-important question of what they would wear – or rather what they elected not to wear. "We definitely used our sexuality to our advantage," Flick told Jeff Simpson, "particularly when it came to dealing with BBC bosses. In show-business, attractiveness is a commodity. We were very aware of what we had, and we used it!"

So the programme now boasted three strands: artists making live appearances, home-made or imported video films, and Pan's People. Not much wonder that for generations, *Top of the Pops* became a must-see television event.

Nineteen sixty-eight also marked the show's 250th edition. It was also the year that John Peel, Radio 1's "underground" star, made his first appearance on *Top of the Pops*. In typically laconic Peel style, he introduced himself as "the one who comes on Radio 1 late at night and plays records made by sulky Belgian art students in basements dying of TB."

Unfortunately, the great man did not fare so well in prime-time, and the fact that he couldn't remember the name of the act he was supposed to be introducing (Amen Corner, as it happens), may explain his absence from the *Pops* studio for the next 14 years! Though writing later, Peel's widow Sheila observed wryly: "It's tempting to wonder if he didn't botch his first *Top of the Pops* appearance… on purpose, rather in the fashion of someone who fluffs dinner so that they won't ever be asked to cook again."

Outside Lime Grove, 1968 was a year marked by assassination and riots. But in *TOTP*-land perhaps the year's most significant event came when Status Quo made their *Top of the Pops* debut. The pile-driving quartet have since entered the record books for having made the most *Top of the Pops* appearances by any group: 86 at the last count!

Quo's drummer, John Coughlan, also remembered the band's *Pops* debut: "Our first appearance was in Manchester with 'Matchstick Men' in 1968 and it was very odd for us. We were very much 'live' and totally nervous about the whole thing. Our parents were watching and that made it doubly pant-wetting for me! Back in those days, the drummers would actually be in *front* of the band …which when you think of it is a bit crazy. Every time I see that clip I can see how completely embarrassed I was… and also how awkward I looked. And later, it was a hoot to be on with our heroes. I was a *major* Jethro Tull fan, and to be on the same show, literally alongside Ian Anderson, was a huge thing for me.

"But the thing to remember is that the whole process was one of mutual respect. The producers liked us, as we always turned up on time. I think they

The Beach Boys in Manchester to record a Pops performance, in November 1964.
Left to right: Al Jardine, Brian Wilson, Carl Wilson, Dennis Wilson, Mike Love

were expecting rock & roll animals, but we were always smartly dressed and treated as friends of the show. Even with the glamorous Legs & Co, there was a mutual respect. There was nothing wild about the *Pops*, it was like any other BBC TV show – planned to perfection and always smooth running."

One particularly memorable *Top of the Pops* appearance came in 1969, when occasional Mick Jagger-squeeze and *Hair* performer Marsha Hunt came on the show to promote her 'Walk On Gilded Splinters'. A spirited performance saw one of Marsha's breasts pop out during the live show. It was another Shock! Horror! TV moment – 7 years before the Sex Pistols, and pre-dating Janet Jackson's 'wardrobe malfunction' by a cool quarter century.

A typical show of that era came in August 1969, when Tony Blackburn introduced the Rolling Stones at No.1 with 'Honky Tonk Women'. Other guests included the Equals ('Viva Bobby Joe'); Zager & Evans ('In the Year 2525'); Love Affair ('Bringing On Back the Good Times'); Bee Gees ('Don't Forget to Remember'); Cilla Black ('Conversations') and... making their only ever *TOTP* appearance, the much-loved Fairport Convention with 'Si Tu Dois Partir' – their (frankly, awful) Cajun-inspired cover of Dylan's 'If You Gotta Go, Go Now'.

Fairport's Richard Thompson admitted to Nigel Schofield: "It wasn't cool to admit it, but everyone secretly wanted to be on *Top of the Pops*... Let's face it, if it was good enough for Hendrix, Cream, the Beatles, Stones and Fleetwood Mac, who was really likely to decline?"

It was that weird combination of armchair favourites appearing on the same show as the Stones and Fairport that so baffled visitors like Tony Visconti. But UK audiences had long been accustomed to such unlikely juxtapositions on Saturday night variety shows: remember Procol Harum on *The Billy Cotton Band Show*?

But gradually, as the 60s progressed, a new line was drawn in the sand. Progressive rock was increasingly at odds with the chart-friendly *TOTP* – although "underground" acts such as Cream, Pink Floyd and Jimi Hendrix were happy enough to appear on the show in the unlikely event that they landed a hit single.

Another such act was Jethro Tull, whose manager had instructed the band's Ian Anderson to "write a quick hit single". Appreciating the irony, Anderson was determined not to take the easy option: "Our first appearance on the show was in early 1969 with 'Living in the Past', which wasn't the easiest tune to play for sure. It was, I think, the first time since Dave Brubeck's 'Take Five' that a 5/4

time signature had been used in a popular song. It was a jazzy groove, and it presented a few problems. It was nerve-wracking to hear the *Pops* orchestra sawing away with us, but adrenalin won the day and it went down great.

"While we were playing, who should be limbering up on the other stage but Cliff Richard, there for his current hit 'Big Ship', and Cliff was attempting to mimic my one-legged pose. It was indeed an off-putting sight, Cliff hobbling around, trying to dance to it on one foot!... But I did get what I had always longed for – an autograph from the man himself: 'To Ian – see you in the charts, love Cliff.' And that, after all, I suppose summed the show up rather nicely!"

The *Old Grey Whistle Test* was still 3 years off, but in 1968 the BBC1 launched *How It Is* (later *How Late It Is*) to cater for the tastes of the student underground audience. The magazine-style show boasted rare TV performances from the Nice, Tyrannosaurus Rex, Fairport Convention and, in March 1969, for their only ever UK television appearance – Led Zeppelin.

* * *

It's a cliché to say that until the 1960s, history was a very black and white affair. But there certainly was something colourful, kaleidoscopic and capering about the Swinging 60s. Tailored suits and smart day dresses quickly gave way to jeans, kaftans and mini skirts – but it was not until 27 November 1968 that *Top of the Pops* took its inaugural plunge into the psychedelic world of colour. Test transmissions for internal use had been piloted in 1967, but it was as the decade came to a close that the Beeb finally took the plunge.

LEFT: The Rolling Stones sample some lavish BBC hospitality, 1964

That first show in colour seemed like a real landmark. It featured Dusty Springfield, Blue Mink, Dave Clark 5, a clip of Kenny Rogers and the First Edition, and that week's No.1 – a song that in many ways signaled the end of pop music as we know it. He had previously put together the Pre-Fab Four (the Monkees), and now Don Kirshner brought us a cartoon band he had created called the Archies – who topped the charts for 5 weeks running with 'Sugar Sugar'.

Another, less instant, act who had been plugging away for 5 years prior to *his* debut on *Top of the Pops* was David Bowie, who at the time straddled the worlds of the underground and the charts. After years of struggle with the Manish Boys and the Lower Third, Bowie finally made his *TOTP* debut on 9 October 1969, promoting 'Space Oddity'. Backed by the Ladybirds and the *TOTP* Orchestra, Bowie manfully wrestled with his stylophone to perform his first hit.

That same show featured Lou Christie, the Hollies, Bobbie Gentry and the Temptations. And if you thought the 60s was all *Sgt Pepper* and *Tommy*, that week's *TOTP* also featured Rolf Harris performing Mrs Thatcher's favourite song, 'Two Little Boys'. Rather chillingly, it would go on to become the very last No.1 of the 1960s.

By the end of that pivotal decade, producers were advising fans who wrote in requesting tickets for a *Top of the Pops* recording not to bother, as they were fully booked for the next 6 months. Not bad going, really, for a programme which was only meant to run for six *shows*!

Three of the biggest stars of the era, Elton John, Marc Bolan and Rod Stewart, at a Top of the Pops *rehearsal in 1972*

CHAPTER 2
The 1970s: Feel the Noize

The new decade launched with a bang: in February 1970, Simon & Garfunkel's all-conquering *Bridge Over Troubled Water* became the first single and LP to be simultaneously No.1 in both the UK and USA. The duo's only appearance on *Top of the Pops* had come four years before, miming to 'I Am A Rock'. This time around, rumour had them arriving at the BBC studio to perform 'Bridge Over Troubled Water', only to be told that they must pre-record the song, then have the *Top of the Pops* Orchestra replicate the studio sounds as the duo mimed their performance. The legendarily meticulous Simon & Garfunkel declined. Another reason suggested for their non-appearance was that Simon & Garfunkel refused to appear on a show where they had to play their beautifully crafted song to an audience of dancing teenagers.

As the new decade began, and *Top of the Pops* entered its seventh year, the power of the brand was by now well established. But the era that the programme now entered was all about change. Perceived wisdom has it that the 70s was the painful hangover that inevitably followed the Swinging 60s. And when you consider that the decade was marked by militant trade unions, 3-day weeks, IRA terrorism, petrol rationing, political extremism, financial insecurity – there may be some truth in that analysis. Even as the decade dawned, there was a sense of change in the air. And with the Beatles splitting very publicly, a new generation was looking for their own idols. The light, disposable apple-cheeked "Pop" was giving way to the more serious, studied and wispily-bearded "Rock".

In February 1970, 4 years on from the Beatles' only live *Top of the Pops* appearance, John Lennon returned with his new partner to perform Plastic Ono Band's 'Instant Karma'. Seated at the piano, the crop-haired John seemed at odds with the hirsute, dressed-up, studio audience. But even more out of kilter was Mrs Lennon: Yoko Ono appeared seated – and, surely a *TOTP* first this – blindfolded by a sanitary towel.

* * *

One man who definitely merits a footnote in the *TOTP* story – if only for sheer hard work – is Tony Burrows. In a February 1970 edition of the show, Burrows appeared no fewer than three times in a single show! He fronted Edison Lighthouse ('Love Grows (Where My Rosemary Goes)'; the Pipkins ('Gimme Dat Ding'); and the Brotherhood Of Man ('United We Stand'). But he obviously still had time and energy to spare, because at the time Burrows was also moonlighting as lead singer with White Plains, whose single 'My Baby Loves Lovin' was also in the charts that week, though not featured on the show – presumably the BBC thought that really would be gilding the lily.

Equally industrious at the start of the 1970s, was the man who would become far and away the biggest UK act of the decade. Elton John made his *Top of the Pops* debut in strangely inauspicious circumstances: despite having signed a solo deal, he was still making pin-money replicating other people's chart hits on those 14/11d budget LPs ("can *you* tell the difference?"), where session men would produce facsimiles of current chart hits to keep impecunious pop fans up-to-date with all the latest sounds.

Elton's first appearance on *Top of the Pops* came early in 1970. He was working as a backing singer and was glimpsed briefly behind Brotherhood of Man and, later, Pickettywitch. But in April that year – the month his breakthrough album, *Elton John,* was released – Elton appeared for the first time in his own right, performing his single 'Border Song' which was marked out as a 'Tip for the Top'. Though talking at the time, he still saw himself more as an albums act: "I'd really like to do a couple of gigs a week, because that's how you sell yourself to people. *Top of the Pops* doesn't really give an idea of what you can do – in fact it gives them a totally wrong impression."

It wasn't until January 1971 that Elton appeared on the show as a chart act in his own right, performing his own hit single. It was 'Your Song' that began that extraordinary career – which, more than 40 years later, rages on.

Plugger Allan James was emphatic about the show's importance to an artist's career: "Never underestimate the importance of *TOTP*... I was looking after

LEFT: John Lennon at the time of his only solo Top of the Pops *appearance, February 1970*

Elton John when 'Song For Guy' entered the charts at No. 40. Elton was in Paris having a 'rest' so the management were not that keen, but producer Robin Nash was adamant. So I called Elton at his apartment and convinced him. He flew back for it.

"He then informed us he had been there for his first hair 'weave', and consequently wanted to wear a cowboy hat for the performance. Robin was not keen as it would shadow his face, but reluctantly agreed. After the performance Elton complained of a throbbing head. We rushed him down to his dressing room and tried to get it off – but it was stuck as the stitches had expanded with the heat!

"We had to wait till he cooled off, and then it loosened enough to let us lift it off. 'If my fans could see me now', said Elton with a grin... 'I look like a blinking match – red on top and white underneath!'"

Ann Mann worked on the programme for a number of years, and one of her memories typifies the excesses of that era: she recalls being flown to Paris for lunch, just so she could *listen* to the new Elton John single! Incredibly though, despite his mega-success in the 70s, it took Elton no fewer than 20 years and 66 releases before he made it to No.1 on his own – with 'Sacrifice' in 1990.

Hindsight is one of the great weapons in the arsenal of history. We now know that if the 1960s was the party, then the 1970s was the decade when we settled the bill and dealt with the aftermath. Militancy replaced idealism; peace & love gave way to pragmatism; and the price of Middle East oil unsettled San Francisco's peace & love vibes... but you wouldn't know any of this, by looking at episodes of *Top of the Pops* from the early 70s.

Instead, the programme boasted the usual mixture of the weird and the wonderful. The late 60s chooglin' rock & roll of Creedence Clearwater Revival spilled over into the new decade, sharing house space with one-hit wonders like Lee Marvin... while Bob Dylan's legendarily mysterious the Band were on chart-nodding terms with Gilbert O'Sullivan. There were pop-tastic hits from Pickettywitch, Mungo Jerry, New Seekers and the Poppy Family, while the underground was represented by Ten Years After, Deep Purple and Fleetwood Mac (Peter Green vintage). Reggae brought Bob & Marcia and Desmond Dekker... Mum and Dad always liked to see Cliff Richard, Roger Whitaker and Andy Williams... while Motown was enjoying a blisteringly classic period ('Tears of a Clown', 'Ain't No Mountain High Enough', 'War', 'Ball of Confusion',

'I'll Be There'...) And all them found a welcome on *Top of the Pops*.

And then, of course, there was Clive Dunn! For many viewers, despite its pioneering musical moments, *Top of the Pops* is indelibly linked to novelty records, which seemed to litter the charts during the 1970s. Deposing Dave Edmunds' 'I Hear You Knocking' in late 1970 came *Dad's Army* stalwart Clive Dunn – and 'Grandad'. Surprisingly, Dunn was actually only 51 when he appeared on *Top of the Pops*, complete with rocking chair, to perform the ultimate in corny ballads; which was co-written – as shurely any fule kno – by Herbie Flowers, whose other claim to rock & roll immortality was *that* bass part on Lou Reed's 'Walk on the Wild Side'.

The first Christmas No.1 of the 70s was another song that somewhat stretched the definition of "pop" music. Benny Hill, then one of the country's top TV comedians, actually had quite a track record as a songwriter. I have fond memories of the EP *Benny Hill's Hit Parade, Volume 1* (the voyeuristic 'Pepys Diary' still makes me smile: "Lord Clarendon walks swiftly on, but naughty Samuel Pepys..."). And so, I'm embarrassed to admit, does 'Ernie (The Fastest Milkman In the West)'. With the rise of feminism and a tidal wave of political correctness looming, Hill eventually fell out of favour. But seeing his cheeky choirboy face relishing lines such as "But a woman's needs are many-fold..." still makes me chuckle. At the time he was pushing 50, and the somewhat reclusive Hill couldn't face singing his hit to a studio full of jiving teenagers, so 'Ernie' was only ever shown as a filmed insert.

With still just three television channels, and home video-recording in its infancy, a popular TV series often provided the platform for chart success. A few years after Hill and Dunn, in 1975, the wartime comedy *It Ain't Half Hot Mum* (from the same creators as *Dad's Army*) gave Don Estelle & Windsor Davies a surprise No.1 with their cover of the Ink Spots' standard 'Whispering Grass'; while that same year, TV cop show *Kojak* gave lollipop-sucking Telly Savalas a UK No.1 with 'If '.

Then there was the just-plain-irritating brigade, who seemed to occupy an inordinate amount of space in the 1970s pop charts: Carl Douglas with his 'Kung Fu Fighting'; Lieutenant Pidgeon's 'Mouldy Old Dough'; Ray Stevens' run of novelty hits; and, most baffling of all, in 1972 came Chuck Berry's only UK No.1, the pointlessly smutty 'My Ding A-Ling'. The man of whom *Q* magazine wrote, from memory: "if rock & roll is a pair of trousers, then

Chuck Berry is the elastic that holds it up." And here was that self-same musical legend smirking his way through *Top of the Pops*. And what was he smirking about? Well, whatever it was, it caused Mary Whitehouse no end of umbrage.

"I was amazed by those British novelty acts," Sparks' Ron Mael told Ian Gittins. "The Wombles impressed me in a particular, slightly peculiar way." But Tammy Wynette wasn't so sure; one plugger remembers the country diva looking round a studio filled with Wombles, Gary Glitter and Max Bygraves and then bursting into tears, and complaining she was on a "goddam freak show"!

But for at least half the audience, the abiding memory of *Top of the Pops* remains the terpsichorean delights of Pan's People. However, Sue Menhenick, who joined the troupe in 1974 had marginally more prosaic memories: "Flick [Colby] *loved* her effects, she was always pushing for it – and occasionally it all went a bit OTT! It was in the Spring of 1975 and we were dancing to Barry White's 'What Am I Gonna Do With You', and dry ice was very much 'in'! There was lots of it on stage, far too much to be honest! The set was polished to perfection and there was a wet residue on the surface from the ice. I was dancing behind Babs – and next thing I knew she had slipped and disappeared from sight. We just carried on of course, and nothing was ever said! Another famous dry ice incident came when we were doing a routine to Steve Miller's 'Rock 'n Me'. There were fake rocks on the set, some steps, a waterfall and... far, far too much dry ice being pumped in from below! All people could see were our heads bobbing above the layer of mist – we couldn't see a thing – but we kept on dancing! Of course we had to do something different every week to be remembered, and costumes had to stand out too. We were doing a routine dressed as fairies on trapezes for the New Seekers' 'You Won't Find Another Fool Like Me', and Flick had dangled fake seaweed from the studio ceiling (as you do) and as we were hoisted higher and higher, so our costumes got entangled with it. It was crazy, but that was the joy of the show – controlled chaos!"

In 2013, a 'treasure trove' of lost Pan's People performances from the 1970s was unearthed by the TV finders Kaleidoscope. Presumed lost for over 40 years, the collection showed the troupe dancing to, among others, Elton John's 'Island Girl'; Cozy Powell's 'Dance With the Devil' and T. Rex's 'Truck On Tyke'.

In addition to the excitement generated by Pan's People, you might be lucky enough to witness a come-hither performance from Lynsey De Paul, or the sultry, snaky Noosha of Fox. Then again, you could find yourself watching James

Galway flute his way through 'Annie's Song'. The great and the good, the high and the mighty, the sexy and the staid… all made their way to the *Pops*.

It seems hard to credit now, but back then there was a clear and quite chippy distinction between 'underground' acts (Pink Floyd, Led Zeppelin, King Crimson) and chart acts. So when Free's 'All Right Now' reached No.1 in 1970, it caused a crisis of conscience – as the song's co-writer, and band's bass player, Andy Fraser explained to Mark Blake in 2012: "It was a hit, but you end up questioning your integrity, standing miming on *Top of the Pops*. Our fan base were male blues fans, and when all the girls started nudging their way into the gigs, the guys got a little peeved. They thought we'd sold out…"

'Selling out' was the very worst accusation you could hurl at a progressive or underground band at the time. In order to avoid the ignominy, Led Zeppelin famously never released a UK single until after they had split; Pink Floyd let a decade elapse between 45s; and Genesis were equally sniffy – their 1973 single 'I Know What I Like' could have been their first hit, but as Tony Banks reflected: "We knew we'd written something that had single potential, although we were a bit embarrassed about it as we weren't supposed to be a singles band. Anyway, Charisma put it out and we refused to go on *Top of the Pops*. We thought that was enough of a stand."

As it transpired, Genesis did not make their *Top of the Pops* debut until 5 years later, when the three-man version watched 'Follow You Follow Me' become their first bona-fide hit. It was a song which the band's chronicler Alan Hewitt called a "rarity in the Genesis canon – an instantly catchy song – one which propelled the band into the Top Ten of the UK charts. It ushered in their first appearance on *Top of the Pops* to the horror of their longstanding fans, who felt perhaps the way members of an exclusive gentlemen's club felt when it was opened up to women."

Another band who crossed the Rubicon of commerciality was the Strawbs, as Dave Cousins remembered: "When Dave Lambert came in, that's when we became a rock band. We had appeared on *Top of the Pops* on their album slot, but 'Lay Down' became a hit. We had been popular on the college circuit, but then we were getting mobbed on stage, and the young girls were parading these banners 'We Love You'. It was all Glam, we even got into the eye shadow… So the college audience disappeared overnight; then the fickle pop audience disappeared! We should never have done it, but it was all part of getting dragged

*Pan's People during a 1971 dance routine.
(Note lunar module and excitable audience)*

along in the excitement. You've come up through the folk clubs and the college circuit, then it's big halls, selling out everywhere and you get carried away."

As well as steamrollering from stadium to stadium with their marathon live shows and best-selling albums, Led Zeppelin enjoyed considerable success in the American market with singles. But such was the deal Peter Grant had cut for the band in the UK, that they were in a position to veto the record company. 'Whole Lotta Love' though edited as an American single, and scheduled for a UK release, was nixed – although ironically, the CCS version of the song went on to become the *Top of the Pops* theme for eight years. Incredibly, given the band's legendary status, when they finally released 'Whole Lotta Love' as a single in 1997, it marked the first-ever Led Zeppelin UK single – a full 17 years after the band split up. A further irony concerning the band who only *ever* made one UK TV appearance, is that 'Moby Dick' from their second album was used as the theme to BBC2's short-lived *Disco 2* programme.

And here's a funny thing... I always loved that the magnificent song 'Friends' – memorably a hit for Arrival (check out their *Pops* performance of January 1970, following the much-loved Blodwyn Pig) – but never knew until writing this book that it was written by Terry Reid... Jimmy Page's first choice as singer with... Led Zeppelin!

One act who seemed relatively comfortable straddling the divide between the underground and the charts was the Who, but their every appearance on *Top of the Pops* seemed to end in some sort of anarchy, usually at the hands of drummer Keith Moon. Jeff Christie, who with his eponymous band created the infectious hits 'Yellow River' and 'San Bernadino', paid regular visits to the *TOTP* studio in the early 1970s.

"One particular memory was, doing the show at the same time as the Who, who were there recording 'The Seeker'," Jeff recalled. "In the final rehearsal before the show, we were waiting for our slot, hanging about on the floor with camera crews and assorted *TOTP* personnel as the Who were taking the stage to rehearse.

"The last to appear was the Moon, who strode energetically up to us, en route to the stage, said 'Hello lads', and planted a real smackeroo of a kiss firmly on the cheek of the lead guitarist, to his utter astonishment, eliciting guffaws all round. The Moon then exclaimed ‹pure renaissance› and proceeded to jump up on the drum riser ready for action. Always ready to rock and shock, he gave us a wink and a grin and then thundered his way through the song!"

The edition of *Top of the Pops* broadcast on 30 September 1971 saw one of the programme's best-remembered performances – Rod Stewart and the Faces, performing 'Maggie May'. With, at Rod's insistence, special guest and long-time fan John Peel "playing" mandolin. Reinforcing the Faces' image as the quintessential lads band, this *TOTP* has them kicking footballs all over the stage, as Peel kept his head down and "played" away. The performance, Dave Lewis wrote later, was "the perfect antidote to the doom and gloom of early 70s Britain with its industrial unrest, terrorist bombings and record unemployment for the post-war era".

In his diary of 1971, Peel found himself during Christmas with the in-laws, managing to catch a repeat of his "performance": "Turned over to see myself playing mandolin with the Faces on *Top of the Pops*. Very funny to sit and watch it again. God bless them for giving us such joy during 1971."

This was effectively the performance that launched Stewart as a superstar; within weeks 'Maggie May' and its parent album, *Every Picture Tells A Story*, would go on to become the first single and LP by a UK act to be simultaneously No.1 in the UK and USA.

Though rather less successful, Ronnie Lane – Rod's colleague from the Faces – also received a warm welcome at Television Centre, as Keith Altham remembered: "Ronnie had left the Faces, and was launching his solo career. He was asked on *Top of the Pops* to promote 'How Come' and at the time was living in a caravan. So Ronnie turns up at TV Centre in this bloody great caravan, and all the commissionaires are looking forward to putting this uppity pop star in his place. Until Ronnie produces a bottle of Scotch, 'Alright lads?' and the caravan is ushered into one of the very rare parking spaces inside the BBC.

"Ronnie was so popular that he once got the commissionaires to tow Rod Stewart's Lamborghini away because Ronnie told them it was occupying producer Johnnie Stewart's parking space!"

Teenage hysteria came to occupy the front pages once again in that period of what seemed like pop's last vestiges of innocence. The Bay City Rollers, Osmond Brothers, David Cassidy, Jackson 5... all generated scenes of near-riot and mass adulation – the likes of which hadn't been seen since Beatlemania.

David Cassidy ruefully reflected: "I was never allowed to perform on *Top of the Pops*, I was told there'd be too many security problems." Certainly whenever word leaked out that, say the Rollers were due at Television Centre, it seemed like most of London W12 ground to a halt! BBC director Stanley Appel remembered "Bay City Rollers fans scaling the walls of Television Centre in their hundreds. Many of the commissionaires were ex-military men, very imposing, but hardly able to chase energetic, enthusiastic teenage fans!"

* * *

In January 1971 the *TOTP* album slot was born, when Tony Blackburn introduced McGuinness Flint performing 'Mister Mister' and 'Dream Darling Dream'. But it turned out to be a short-lived segment – with the final installment coming just 9 months later, in the show aired on the 23 September 1971 – which featured the Carpenters singing a cover of 'Help!' as well as 'Superstar'.

In 1968 LP sales had overtaken those of singles for the first time, and that was certainly one factor in the programme's decision to introduce an album slot. But the final decision was made while Johnnie Stewart was away in the United States. His replacement on the show, Stanley Dorfman, decided that an album slot would more fully reflect the pop landscape of the time – but on his return, Stewart nixed it, on the basis that "it bore no relation to the charts at all…"

Among the acts who appeared in the album slot while it lasted, were Murray Head & Yvonne Elliman, who in April came along to promote the shocking new double concept LP, *Jesus Christ, Superstar*. Tony Blackburn, somewhat improbably, introduced Caravan performing the title track of their second album, 'If I Could Do It All Over Again…' In July 1971, Fairport Convention, still reeling from Richard Thompson's departure, were on to push *Angel Delight*. And, on that same show, just watch Polly Brown leading Pickettywitch through the naggingly insistent 'Chirpy Chirpy Cheep Cheep', and what a voice she had – hypnotic… Robotic even! She could have replaced Nico in the Velvet Underground – or, here's a thought, joined Kraftwerk… And those fashions: hot pants for the ladies, and – 'suits you sir' – cravats for the gentlemen!

* * *

On New Year's Eve 1971, hot-foot from Radio 1, Ed 'Stewpot' Stewart arrived: "So there I was, live on the show for the very first time. And having grazed my eye with a contact lens a few days before, I was horror stricken to discover I would have to wear a patch to protect it… Just what I needed! But although I didn't feel particularly sexy at the time, I was actually doing rather well with the ladies, and weirdly two of them were on that same show! I was seeing Eve Graham of the New Seekers who appeared singing 'I'd Like to Teach the World to Sing', and I was *also* seeing Babs from Pan's People who were, of course, on the show too – mind you neither had the faintest idea about the other! I have always had an eye for the ladies it has to be said; but on *that* day I had exactly that!"

By 1971 *Top of the Pops* had been on the air for 7 years, and over that period there had been major changes in the Pantheon of Pop. It was clear now that the Beatles were no longer a functioning group; the Rolling Stones had slipped away into tax exile; Bob Dylan had gone into hiding; while Jimi Hendrix, Janis Joplin, Brian Jones and Jim Morrison were no more... The old guard was gone, and the audiences who flocked to the *TOTP* studio every week, and the millions watching at home, badly needed some new stars of their own...

"Glam rock was the first and last musical genre that was solely created on, and because of, *Top of the Pops*," Jeff Simpson wrote later. "If the show hadn't existed, there would have been no Glam Rock."

Legend has it that when, in April 1971, Marc Bolan's T.Rex got to No.1 for the first time, with 'Hot Love', Bolan – determined to make an impact on the programme – threw some glitter on his cheeks. The next day, make-up counters across the country were besieged and soon sold out of glitter! Thus was glam rock born...

As a leading light of the 60s underground, many fans felt betrayed by Bolan the boppin' elf's defection to the pop charts. Ripped from the verdant pastures of Tolkien and the childhood realms roamed by Tyrannosaurus Rex, the chart-topping TV stars T.Rex seemed a betrayal. Bolan biographer Mark Paytress remembers T.Rex appearing at the Weeley Festival Of Progressive Music in 1971, alongside Lindisfarne, the Faces, Quintessence and Colosseum. The headlining Bolan was getting a hard time from the crowd of heads who heckled his band: "I'm Marc Bolan," he said at one point, "you've probably seen me on *Top of the Pops*." But that programme was the antithesis of progressive music and the heckling persisted.

Lest we forget, Gary Glitter was also a huge star of the glam era. Born Paul Gadd, at the time he made his *TOTP* debut in 1972, Paul Raven (aka Paul Monday) was best-known as the warm-up man for *Ready! Steady! Go!*

Glam Rock in excelsis: Marc Bolan (LEFT), August 1972 and Slade's Noddy Holder, November 1972

Now, reborn in bacofoil as 'Gary Glitter' (the Liberace of the glam scene) he seemed like a parody of the Bolan and Bowie brigade. It all began with a cancelled David Essex session, when Glitter – together with writer and producer Mike Leander – fashioned the floor-stomping favourite 'Rock & Roll, Part II', he created a monster, that went on to enjoy eight Top Ten hits and three separate No.1s.

Of all the 70s acts who claimed to have made it "as big as the Beatles", Slade probably came the closest. The Black Country quartet scored an incredible six No.1s between 1971 and 1973! They also became the first act ever to have three singles enter the charts at the top! Not even the Fab Four managed that – and symbolically, 'Cum On Feel the Noize' was the first single to enter at No.1 since 'Get Back' 4 years before.

Memorable as those catchy Slade singles were, the band's *Top of the Pops* appearances were equally unforgettable. Noddy Holder: a larger than life frontman, complete with bushy sideboards straight out of Dickens, top-hat, and paint-stripping voice. Equally striking was guitarist Dave Hill, who soon realised that to grab the camera's attention he had to make himself look outstanding, and boy, did he relish the challenge.

As Noddy Holder told Jeff Simpson: "It all got out of hand with the bands like Sweet and Gary Glitter trying to outdo each other... But Dave Hill wasn't having any of that. He wanted to be more and more outrageous every time he appeared. He used to go into the toilet to get dressed, so we never saw his outfits until he'd got the whole regalia on... He'd come out and we'd fall about... laughing at whatever he'd got on. His favourite saying was 'You write 'em, I'll sell 'em!'"

Dave himself agreed: "Being on the show was, of course, about the music, but with bands like us, it was always about 'the look', and being as OTT as possible! I would always like to surprise the band with what I was going to wear. It's actually true that people would tune in to see what gear I was in: the top-hat... the silver or gold boots... it was all part of the selling of Slade.

"On the day of the show I would pop into Kensington Market to see what was new in. I was often served by a certain Freddie Mercury who was working there. Who could have known! When colour came to TV land, we were there to take full advantage of it on the show. It was a turning point for pop really... and we went for the glitter and glam look big time! Showbiz had come *alive*!

The thrill of being on the *Pops* was never bigger than on occasions when you filmed on location away from the studio. I will never forget shooting a promo for 'Get Down And Get With It' at Battersea Power Station in 1971 – it was *so* exciting. But the real thrill came from sitting down with the whole family to watch the show together. That was the essence of the *Pops* – it bought different generations together like no pop show before or since!"

Noddy Holder had begun his professional career as a roadie for Hobstweedle – one of Robert Plant's pre-Led Zeppelin outfits. He only got the gig because his dad was a window cleaner and Noddy was allowed to drive his van! Despite their cheery, beery singalong hits and well-deserved reputation as a powerhouse live attraction, the band freely acknowledged that it was *Top of the Pops* which really established them nationally.

"It was the show that broke us wide open," Noddy stated emphatically. "Simple as that!" While David Bowie and Marc Bolan were effectively solo stars, Slade were always a group – and as such, they inherited and held the Beatle mantle for 2 years until the end of 1973. The final Slade No.1 was the timeless 'Merry Xmas Everybody'. A festive perennial, it has been a UK chart hit *ten* times since its original 1973 release. And in this era of downloads, it is perhaps worth recalling that in those distant days Slade's 'Merry Xmas Everybody' racked up advance orders of half a million – and on its first day of release, the single sold 300,000 copies.

In the wake of Bowie, Bolan, Slade and Glitter came Roxy Music – offering avant-garde rock & roll for the 1970s. The band made their *TOTP* debut in August 1972, promoting 'Virginia Plain' – one of the all-time great debut singles. "If ever one needed proof of how a band had cut the emotional and sartorial umbilical chord between performer and audience," wrote Roxy's biographer David Buckley, "there was it. The band looked like it had been beamed down not only from another era, but also from another planet altogether. This was Dr Who pop for the *Dr Who* generation." Fronted by the effortlessly stylish Bryan Ferry, Roxy also boasted the androgynous Eno.

A further Roxy performance, of 'Street Life' on the programme in 1973, "reduced the teenies to matchwood" wrote Jon Savage. It was undeniably the era of style over content, and few acts epitomized that more than Roxy Music: "Other bands wanted to wreck hotel rooms," Bryan Ferry laughed later, "Roxy Music wanted to redecorate them!"

But of the all the acts of that era, it was David Bowie's 'Starman' which stands as probably the best-loved and most influential *Top of the Pops* appearance of all time.

Bowie had unveiled Ziggy Stardust in the rather insalubrious surroundings of the Toby Jug, Tolworth in February 1972, immediately prior to the release of his fifth album – the perennially popular *Rise & Fall Of Ziggy Stardust*. 'Starman' had crept out the following April, and even Ziggy's TV debut that June (on *Lift Off With Ayshea*) hadn't help propel it up the charts. Following a show the night before at the Rainbow Pavilion in Torquay, Bowie and the Spiders repaired to London for their make or break TV appearance.

It was 5 July 1972, when an other-worldly Bowie gazed out from his discordant eyes into the BBC cameras, singing about a far-out alien. Most of those watching the carrot-haired, alligator-suited, Bowie assumed the song to be autobiographical – perhaps he really had come from outer space, rather than Beckenham in Kent... In all the show's 8-year history, no one had *ever* looked that *weird*. And as the song's plaintive melody progressed, Bowie nonchalantly draped an arm round the shoulders of peroxide guitarist Mick Ronson. The singer smirked – he knew exactly what he was doing; the guitarist looked embarrassed. And la la la, 'Starman' set forth for unknown galaxies and, wham, bam – a star was born.

Elton John, the UK's biggest-selling star of the 1970s, performing 'Daniel' on TOTP in January 1973

In his grippingly comprehensive *The Complete David Bowie*, Nicholas Pegg wrote: "More than any other individual performance, it was this one iconic television spot... which catapulted Bowie to stardom. It's deceptively easy to forget that in the summer of 1972, David Bowie was still yesterday's news to the average viewer of *Top of the Pops*, a one-hit wonder who'd had a novelty single about an astronaut at the end of the previous decade. Three minutes on *Top of the Pops* in a rainbow jumpsuit and shocking red hair put paid to that forever."

'Starman' began that run of classic David Bowie singles which so dominated the charts between 1972 and 1974 – the Ziggy and Aladdin era. Then came the Thin White Duke; then the Berlin trilogy... No wonder that *New Musical Express* voted Bowie as the most influential artist of the millennium... And it had all started with three minutes of 'hazy cosmic jive' one Thursday night on *Top of the Pops*.

Future *GQ* editor Dylan Jones wrote a whole *book* about that epochal moment; while future pop stars Marc Almond, Gary Kemp, Holly Johnson, Ian McCulloch and Gary Numan have all testified to the impact of that transfiguring performance.

Intriguing, and often overlooked, is the fact that between 'Space Oddity' and 'Starman', Bowie had also managed to sneak in another *TOTP* appearance. June 1971 found him playing piano behind Peter Noone, the former Herman of the Hermits, who was beginning a solo career with a cover of Bowie's 'Oh You Pretty Thing'. In fact, that No.12 hit also effectively marked the *end* of Noone's solo career.

The rivalry between acts continued off camera as well, as Bryan Ferry remembered in 2013: "You'd do *Top of the Pops* and find out what your status was. Elton John would get a dressing room to himself and a few for his band, while Roxy, and even Bowie, would get squashed into a tiny room. Then there would be a fight over bar tickets. Only certain bands would get a pass to the BBC bar to get free drinks afterwards. It was fun. They were creative times. We were friends and we were rivals."

'Starman' aside, another classic Bowie *TOTP* appearance from the 70s made headlines in 2012. The footage belonged to TV cameraman John Henshall, who hadn't realised how rare the performance was. The four-minute clip showed Bowie performing alongside his then-band The Spiders From Mars, who play a slightly extended version of 'Jean Genie'. The performance has not been broadcast on TV since it originally aired on 4 January 1973, the day after it was recorded.

Henshall who worked on the show, had kept a copy of Bowie's appearance. He mentioned the tape during an interview on Johnnie Walker's Radio 2 show in 2012, after which excited Bowie aficionados contacted him to explain its rarity value. "I just couldn't believe that I was the only one with it. I just thought you wouldn't be mad enough to wipe a tape like that," said Henshall.

Mark Cooper, executive producer of *Top of the Pops 2*, said: "Bowie singing 'The Jean Genie' is electric and the kind of piece of archive that not only brings back how brilliant *Top of the Pops* could be, but also how a piece of archive can speak to us down the years. I can't imagine what other piece of *TOTP* from the early Seventies would be as extraordinary a find."

Over the years, the BBC's policy of wiping some of their vintage television programmes has come in for heavy and persistent criticism. It is estimated that of those first 500 editions of *Top of the Pops*, only 20 complete programmes survive.

The BFI's TV expert, Dick Fiddy, who has kept a close eye on the Corporation's attitude over the years told me: "When you wiped something, you went to the producer, and certain producers didn't want their stuff wiped… [But] they generally said yes, because those producers were in the business of making television: getting on with the next job and not worrying about the last job.

"Contracts were very weird, they usually gave you a 3-year window and after those 3 years, it couldn't be shown again without re-negotiation, which was costly. In some areas, the copyright owners insisted on the content being destroyed… Music copyright has become a nightmare over the years; for years, *Top of the Pops* repeats were far easier, but then the business got big…

"Because music was such a big business, and huge amounts of money were rolling in, the record companies realised very, very quickly that TV exposure provided an enormous boost. It was becoming – certainly by the end of the 60s – bigger than radio exposure. And an appearance on *Top of the Pops* moved your record up the charts. It delivered an enormous amount of money… It was an alliance which made everyone happy: the BBC got a – relatively – cheap programme; the record companies got this huge financial boost; and the stars got exposure.

"The earliest surviving episode is the 1964 Christmas Special, with Diana Ross. But tracking down the surviving *Top of the Pops*, is very tricky. A lot of those performances were sold on to foreign television programmes – now they perhaps didn't wipe that performance with the same diligence as the BBC, so they survived longer. Thirty or 40 years down the line, the Swedes, Dutch, Germans or whoever, own these programmes but don't realise they're bought-in material. So more survive than in the official archive.

"And that's the other thing: music TV was so popular, so all-pervading for that generation, that people kept copies when they weren't supposed to. If you were an engineer and a fan of Dusty Springfield or Jimi Hendrix, and were told to wipe that tape, you might think, hang on, and keep a copy for yourself before you wiped it.

"And then there are the copies which were recorded at home – the very rich of those days, who could afford home recorders, were the pop stars. Now they were often touring, and would have taped *Top of the Pops* because they'd be on tour or recording in the studio.

"By about 1977–78 things had changed, tapes were becoming cheaper, there were different ways to keep tape and the BFI started to have a co-ordinated archive to keep material. When the BBC started to dump stuff we would say 'Oh, we'll have that!' And then the technology starts to change: tape moves from 2" to 1", then the switch to digital... So the tapes become useless, and there's less value in wiping them because they're not looking to be used again.

"When *Top of the Pops* began, you have Ken Dodd and semi-operatic Engelbert, some American folkies, a great eclectic mix, and that's because it was evolving. But that's gone by the end of the 70s. With a couple of obvious novelty exceptions, what you got then is music from definite genres – glam, pop, rock, punk... Through its life, *Top of the Pops* has had a couple of crises, and perhaps the most important is the devaluation of the pop charts. In the early 70s, you could argue that the album charts were a lot more interesting than the singles charts, album bands stop doing singles, people are doing *Tubular Bells*, so what you get is not perhaps the best artists on *Top of the Pops* because they're not making singles."

✳ ✳ ✳

Wherever you stood on the pop spectrum, underground or overground (or, indeed, Wombling free), not everyone was enamoured at being on the show. Mott the Hoople's Overend Watts told the band's biographer Campbell Devine:

"*Top of the Pops* was absolute hell! You had to get there for 10 in the morning, but they didn't need you... Then about one o'clock you'd go up for a camera angle rehearsal. They'd play the record and you stood there while the producer sorted out the cameramen... that took half an hour, then you'd go back to your room and you couldn't get out of the building... At four o'clock you came down for a dress rehearsal and ran through the song, miming, before you came back down again and did the filming at seven or eight o'clock. Then without fail, after every show, you would want to go to the BBC bar for a drink, and the old blokes with caps wouldn't let you because you weren't a BBC Club member." Such trenchant feelings may well have accounted for the snide reference to *Top of the Pops* on Mott's 'Saturday Gigs' hit.

Coming in on the back of glam rock, Mott were memorably described as 'hod-carriers in drag'. They first appeared on *Top of the Pops* in August 1972, promoting their gift from David Bowie: 'All the Young Dudes'. (They were originally offered 'Suffragette City', but declined). Busy touring, the band later splashed out a grand total of £150 on a promo video to be played on the show for their own follow-up to 'Dudes', 'Honaloochie Boogie'!

The much-loved Mott went on to be regular visitors on the show – one memorable appearance had Tony Blackburn introducing the band – with the help of a visiting Womble – as they went through a clenched-teeth version of 'Roll Away the Stone'... It was, indeed, a mighty long way down rock & roll.

Robin Nash took over as the programme's producer in 1973, with a CV which included *Dixon of Dock Green, Crackerjack* and that temperamental showbiz dynamo, *Basil Brush*. It was on Nash's watch that the first accusations of chart-fixing occurred. The all-important Top Twenty had long been compiled by the trade paper *Record Retailer* (which later became *Music Week*) ringing round record shops to log sales. *Music Week* then teamed up with the British Phonographic Industry (BPI) and engaged the new-fangled computers of the British Market Research Bureau (BRMB) to compile a more reliable reflection of the nation's record-buying tendencies. But it soon became apparent that some unscrupulous types, employed by the major labels, had identified which shops were being used to compile the chart – and soon, rumours of hyping and chart-rigging were circulating.

In those happy, far-off days before we all learned to be drink-aware, *TOTP* was fuelled by alcohol, as plugger Richard ('The Plumber') Evans recalled:

"There were plenty of drinks knocking about back then, Robin Nash would be striding about with a pint glass perpetually filled with Vodka & Tonic by us promo people – that was our job! Buying drinks was a massive part of our job. Then Decca boss David Rickerby would give me *mounds* of cash and tell me... 'Don't come back till you get an act on *Top of the Pops*!'"

In 1973 the Who were invited to promote their new single '5.15', taken from *Quadrophenia*, on the 500th edition of *Top of the Pops*. And, in typical Who fashion, Moon destroyed his drum kit while Townshend did his best to smash his guitar. However, such was the upset, that the destruction was edited out of the programme before it was broadcast the following night, and the band was banned from the show. They would not reappear on *Top of the Pops* until March 1981, when they mimed to 'You Better You Bet'.

✳ ✳ ✳

It was a right rum old time, the 70s: an unsettling combination of 3-day weeks, flared trousers and international terrorism. And it also threw up some of the unlikeliest stars ever to appear on *Top of the Pops*. We had to wait a few more years for the Fagin-like presence of Ian Dury, but 1974 did provide us with the sight of lovable old leftie, and future national treasure, Robert Wyatt on the programme. The former Soft Machine drummer had been paralysed from the waist down in an accident the year before, but thanks to the support of colleagues in the music industry, he had persevered with his musical career. It was a tongue-in-cheek cover of the Monkees' 'I'm a Believer' that landed Wyatt his *TOTP* slot in September that year.

Behind the scenes, there were worries that the sight of a man in a wheelchair on the teenagers' favourite show might be unsettling – so Wyatt was offered the use of Val Doonican's rocking chair instead! Understandably, he declined; his appearance on the show hurtled his single up to No. 29; and the cool types viewing at home – though probably *not* the teen audience bopping in the studio – had great fun identifying his backing band. Wasn't that Pink Floyd's Nick Mason on drums? And Henry Cow's Fred Frith on guitar; Hatfield & the North's Richard Sinclair on bass; and Matching Mole's Dave Sinclair on keyboards? Surely this was the biggest collection of pop avant garde ever gathered together – at least outside of the *Old Grey Whistle Test* studio!

And just in case you are worrying about that rejected rocking chair... Never fear: it had already seen many years of good service. It was occupied by Clive Dunn when he was on *Top of the Pops* singing 'Grandad'; it had featured on the cover of the LP *Val Doonican Rocks… But Gently*; and it was also employed on Michael Holiday's 1963 TV series, and *The Morecambe & Wise Show*.

✳ ✳ ✳

During the 1970s, it was open house on *Top of the Pops* – the folk-rock sensation Lindisfarne (another 'new Beatles', if memory serves) raided the BBC props department for silly costumes when they were on the show to promote 'Meet Me on the Corner'. And as Lindisfarne bassist Rod Clements confirmed: "Being on *Top of the Pops* gave you a sense of having arrived; it was a definite feather in your cap". Other acts from the folk-rock firmament who appeared on the show at the time included the aforementioned Strawbs; East Of Eden with their instrumental 'Jig A Jig'; singer-songwriters Don McLean, Gordon Lightfoot and Buffy Saint-Marie; as well as the soft rock offerings from America and Bread.

At the beginning of their career, Thin Lizzy enjoyed a hit with a rocky reworking of the traditional folk song 'Whiskey in the Jar'. Phil Lynott's power trio were invited over from Dublin soon after, and guitarist Eric Bell described it vividly: "The first time we appeared on *Top of the Pops*, well, for a start we genuinely couldn't believe it, hardly any Irish bands had ever been on the show up until then. I just remember what looked like a large warehouse, with little round stages everywhere all over the floor.

"Then we saw this guy marching toward us. He had on a black polo-neck with a gold chain and medallion around his neck. He came over and barked: 'Which lot are you?' We told him rather nervously who we were. 'And which one of you is the drummer?' So, Brian Downey, rather baffled, said 'I'm the drummer.' 'Well,' said the guy 'I hope you're not like that dreadful drummer from the Who. They were here last week and the mess they made, he kicked his drums off the stage, there were drums everywhere…!' And with that, he minced away".

One of the most striking performers of the era was Alvin Stardust. Today Alvin is best remembered for his mean and moody *TOTP* performances – the black-clad leather look came about completely by accident, the leather gloves were only there to cover the stains made by his hair-dye! "I felt pretty silly throughout the show," Alvin laughed, "we just played at pop, we acted out a part and everyone seemed to love it.

The Sweet give it some Wig-Wam Bam in September 1972

"On my first show Tony Blackburn was presenting, and I was desperate that no-one find out that I had been Shane Fenton in another life. I thought that I might be seen as a 60s rocker, and they wouldn't play my records. So I walked into the studio with four big bouncers who had orders that no-one was to talk to me. Tony walks up and says 'Hi Alvin, did you...' and the bouncers walked me off and back to the dressing room. That is how I got the 'mean and moody' reputation, and how I got the nickname 'The Untouchable'.

"Producer Robin Nash gave me a strange but very true piece of advice. When 'My Coo-Ca-Choo' was at No. 2 in the chart, he took me to one side and said: 'Let's hope it doesn't get to No.1 my boy.' When I asked why, he said: 'Well, if your first single tops the charts everything that follows will be seen as a disappointment!' Well it stayed at 2, then the follow up 'Jealous Mind' got to the top, and that was my only chart topper. But I didn't mind too much as I did okay after that.

"Robin would get really annoyed at Mike Mansfield over at *Supersonic* on ITV, as he would always open the show shouting 'Cue camera six!' He, like Robin, only had three cameras, but was just having a dig. Robin *hated* it!

"But the power of the show was global! When I was in Japan for the first time, the chairman of the record company met me at the airport shouting "Ah, welcome Mister Stardust, I watch you on *Top of the Pops*!"

Looking back on some of those *Top of the Pops* episodes in the 70s, there was definitely a sense of kids raiding the dressing-up cupboard. Mud, Queen, the Sweet, Gary Glitter, Wizzard, Slade, Elton, Roxy Music and Bowie all seemed to regard it as a challenge to appear in the most outrageous get-up on a Thursday night. Mind you, there was some strong competition from the Goodies, Smurfs and Bryan & Michael.

And, of course, those regular visitors to the *TOTP* studio, all the way from Wimbledon... the Wombles enjoyed four Top Ten hits during 1974 alone, and because of the strict Musicians' Union ruling on performances, real musicians had to record the backing tracks, even if it was for a furry group. Among those who later admitted to spending time inside a Womble costume are Steeleye Span and future Sex Pistols producer, Chris Spedding!

Wimbledon's strongest competition at the time came from outside the UK – Abba made their *Top of the Pops* debut in 1974 after storming to victory in the Eurovision Song Contest with the catchy 'Waterloo'. Besides their innate ability at creating pop perfection, the Swedish quartet also benefitted from being extremely photogenic. Abba enjoyed nine UK No.1 singles between 1974 and 1980. And if the group themselves couldn't make it to the *Pops* studio, they always ensured that a striking video was ready to be screened – remember the Bergman-esque 'Mamma Mia'?

Even when their run of beguiling pop hits finally came to an end, the Abba phenomenon simply refused to die. Erasure's *Abba-Esque* was an old-fashioned EP which reached UK No.1 in 1992; Steps' medley 'Thank Abba for the Music' was a 1999 UK No. 2; the 2008 film of *Mamma Mia!* became the most successful musical ever released in the UK; *Abba Gold* became the best-selling CD album ever released in the UK with more than 4 million sales; Madonna sampled Abba; U2 paid homage to Abba; and the money on the table for an Abba reunion in the 21st Century would have settled Third World debt…

* * *

Of all the BBC's DJs over the years, one of the most-respected remains Johnnie Walker – currently still on the coal-face at Radio 2. But incredibly, despite all his years at Broadcasting House, Johnnie only ever presented *Top of the Pops* once, in January 1974. As he told Shaun Tilley: "I got a call that afternoon from my agent, somebody had dropped out, and I felt an immediate stab of fear, because I hadn't really done much TV. But if you're going to do television, start off small, some late-night thing that nobody watches, but here I was going to present *Top of the Pops*! I was *very* nervous, and when I get nervous, I tend to frown, and my eyes get frighteningly scary!

"Part of the reason I got into radio is that I can hide away when I do it. The regular *Pops* presenters – Tony Blackburn, Noel Edmonds – were more extrovert. I used to do the chart rundown on Radio 1 on Tuesday afternoon, so it's quite surprising I *didn't* do it more. To be honest with you, I thought the show was a bit naff… I loved some of the pop, but on my daytime show I'd be playing album music. I'd come from the freedom of the pirate stations.

"*Ready! Steady! Go!* was a great TV show, packed with people, let's create a club, get over great American acts – the Four Tops, Otis Redding, Jerry Lee Lewis – a fantastic show, great atmosphere, whereas *Top of the Pops* was manufactured for TV. The atmosphere in the studio was non-existent, the audience look bored, I'm sure they had applause tracks on, because there were only ever about 20 people in the audience!"

Despite the success of the Scandinavian marauders, in Britain during 1975 the biggest name was… Mud. The quartet spent 45 weeks on the UK singles chart that year – not much wonder that during a visit to record their Christmas appearances, Mud spent most of their off-camera time signing 10,000 autographs for their fans!

While Mud were at the top, one act later to become a regular visitor to the *TOTP* studio was just making his debut. Midge Ure: "My first ever *Top of the Pops* was on New Year's Eve 1975, when they decided to give four unknown bands with new releases a spot on the programme. Slik was one of those four. It took us aback to find out how small the studio was, and how ridiculously young the audience was. I had watched the show since it was first broadcast and couldn't quite comprehend how different it was being there.

"After the recording, we jumped on the overnight train back to Glasgow. But it might as well have been a time machine or some form of 'space age' transporter, because once the New Year's Day show was broadcast, we could have been living on another planet. We were recognised in the street! Everyone wanted to know us – the opposite sex even found us strangely attractive! That was the power that *TOTP* had. It elevated you to a level you could only ever dream of attaining. You had arrived and felt like you belonged to a very exclusive club."

For all the hysteria generated by the pop acts, and the mayhem caused by Keith Moon, the still rather staid BBC preferred their musicians to be house-trained, and miming was one way of controlling them. The whole miming issue was one that baffled the musicians, but such was the power of the trades unions during the 1970s that everyone abided by their rules. All the musicians who played on those original recordings had to replicate that performance on tape in the *Top of the Pops* studio – backed, if necessary, by the *TOTP* Orchestra. That would be the version an act would then have to mime to on that week's show. Although never popular with the artists themselves, the orchestra lasted until 1980, when – irony of ironies – a Musicians' Union strike led to it being dropped.

On the subject of miming, just look at Deep Purple mugging through 'Black Night' in 1970: could anyone look more bored than organist Jon Lord? Could anyone mime more obviously than drummer Ian Paice? But when it comes to miming, you should always check out the drummer – who will either be giving it far more effort than the song requires, or else sitting there looking jaded, bored beyond belief, and tip-tapping away, like your Dad reluctantly roped in for Saturday afternoon's DIY.

Queen was one band who managed to become synonymous with *Top of the Pops* – primarily for not being there! In their absence, the 1975 video of 'Bohemian Rhapsody' effectively launched not only an entire music video industry and a worldwide TV network, but the very way which we now look at pop music. They had actually made their *TOTP* debut the previous year, even before 'Seven Seas Of Rhye' – their second single and first hit – appeared in the shops. When another band dropped out leaving a space in that week's show, EMI's promotional department received a panic phone call from the *Pops'* producer Robin Nash – and Queen rushed to Pete Townshend's studio to record a backing track which they performed on the 21 February 1974 edition of the show, two days before the single reached the shops. At the time, Freddie Mercury didn't even have a TV set, so he ended up watching his television debut in a shop window on Oxford Street!

Over the years Queen made a number of unforgettable *Top of the Pops* performances, and supplied a host of equally memorable videos. But the one that everyone remembers is, of course, 'Bohemian Rhapsody'. A buzz was already building around the six-minute single and it was inevitable that Queen would be asked onto the show to promote it, but they were already locked into a lengthy pre-Xmas UK tour. And so it was on 10 November 1975, during a pre-tour rehearsal at Elstree Studios, that on a whim the band asked director Bruce Gowers (who had directed their earlier *Live at the Rainbow* film) to shoot a short promotional film. His video brought the cover of *Queen II* to life, and during a four-hour shoot at a grand total of £4,500, Gowers oversaw the birth of the rock video – which certainly marked an improvement on the little films the BBC previously produced.

Long-time *TOTP* associate Stanley Appel: "We used to have a Friday afternoon surgery; the pluggers would come in with their records, all appointments were booked, thus, 'the surgery'. That gave you an idea of what might chart, but Sunday afternoon of course was the chart rundown, which dictated that week's content.

"Quite often you might find an American act had a hit, and would not be available to get to London for the Thursday recording, so I'd be sent out with a camera and small crew to shoot something – they weren't particularly distinguished! I remember Norman Greenbaum's 'Spirit in the Sky': lots of skyscrapers, and a *lot* of clouds…"

And talking of clouds… Producer Robin Nash was quick to realise that Judy Collins' 1975 single of Stephen Sondheim's 'Send in the Clowns' (which the composer modestly calls "*the* hit") was destined for chart greatness. Robin had in mind a lavish staircase down which Judy would descend, but when he arrived in the studio he was surprised to find a backdrop designed to accompany 'Send in the *Clouds*'!

One man who would later become a regular visitor remembered his first visit to the hallowed ground. "It was back in the days when the show came from Lime Grove in West London," recalled Pete Waterman, "and it was in 1975 that I had my first hit with Susan Cadogan and 'Love Me Baby'.

"It was very, very strange back then as we would all sit on chairs waiting to be called in to do a 're-record' of the track in question. You'd be sitting with a Bryan Ferry or a David Essex, waiting your turn! And you had to behave, no messing about! It was like being back in school assembly! But everyone, – like Johnnie Stewart – was generally nice to you, it was just a bit regimented!

"There was a fabulous occurrence in 1975 with Pete Shelley doing 'Love Me, Love My Dog'. Someone thought it would be a great idea for Pete to have a Dulux dog on the set with him while he was singing, and everyone thought it would be OK as it was on a lead. To keep the dog focused his bone had even been spiked with aniseed! But as the song was finishing, a stage-hand thought it would be good to clear the bone out of shot, and as he threw it – so the dog followed it, complete with Pete – who simply disappeared from sight amidst thumps and crashes! Ah, the magic of *Top of the Pops*!

"It was amazing how powerful that show was, particularly on sales. Rick Astley had been heard all over the radio, but when he was on the show everyone was amazed how the look was so different to his sound, and sales doubled overnight! Such was the amazement at Musical Youth that their sales *trebled*!"

Pan's People's final appearance on *Top of the Pops* came in April 1976, when they danced to 'Silver Star' by the Four Seasons. Flick Colby continued to choreograph the new dance troupe – the unfortunately-named Ruby Flipper. But the novel boy/girl line-up didn't last long. The audience preferred the girls, and there were even suggestions of internal unhappiness at the BBC about the inter-racial nature of the troupe. Whatever the reasons, Ruby Flipper flipped out after only 6 months, to be replaced by the more audience (and BBC management) friendly Legs & Co.

By the mid-70s their routines were becoming decidedly more risque, but the show remained a staple of pre-watershed family viewing, so Legs & Co. couldn't go too far. The *Top of the Pops* running-time was a firmly established half-hour – and whichever acts couldn't be enticed to the studio would be represented by screening a video – and, if that failed, there was always Legs & Co. Some of their more memorable routines included: 'I Can't Stand the Rain' (plastic mac, splashing around in water); 'Typically Tropical' (air hostesses strip to reveal bikinis beneath); 'Egyptian Reggae' (girls dress as a camel); 'Ca Plane Pour Moi' (girls carry baguettes) and, classically, 'Bank Robber' (girls carry bags marked 'Swag').

"I thought having the dance troupes on was becoming a bit clichéd, it was like saying well we'll get the girls to dance because we can't get the group in the studio...", reflected *TOTP* presenter Andy Peebles.

The early 1970s found certain musicians increasingly flexing their creative muscles, with albums like *Tubular Bells, Dark Side of the Moon* and *The Yes Album*. But, at the same time, the chart-friendly *Top of the Pops* is perhaps best remembered for its 1970s incarnation – a fact that is supported by the viewing figures.

There was still plenty of room on the show for engaging one-off hits; there was room for singles embracing disco, reggae, country; there were pop remakes like Gary Shearston's suave cover of 'I Get A Kick Out Of You' and Prelude's haunting acappella take on 'After the Goldrush'. There was also the smoothly-polished pop of 10cc; the brass band appeal of Peter Skellern; the road-weary Lobo and his dog named Boo; Sparks' and their sinister Fuhrer-lookalike pianist; Leo Sayer's pierrot; retro rock & roll from the Rubettes; and Uncle Tom Cobley and all...

Showaddywaddy were another major act in the mid-70s, racking up ten Top Ten singles, including a 1974 No.1 with 'Under the Moon of Love'. Such success obviously guaranteed regular *Top of the Pops* slots, as singer Dave Bartram testified: "Our first appearance was in May 1974 with our debut hit 'Hey Rock & Roll' ... unforgettable! We were *so* excited. We left Leicester at the crack of dawn and arrived as excited as anyone could be, we were like school kids.

"But what we actually walked into was an industrial dispute – the scene shifters were at war, and we were not even allowed to take any equipment in –

The Bay City Rollers pose for a photograph after their Top of the Pops *debut with 'Keep On Dancing', September 1971*

nothing. So our big day consisted of miming with no instruments on the Morecambe & Wise set with *that* kitchen in the background. I was jumping all over a sofa... Totally surreal, and one to remember for sure!

"We loved the whole day at the *Pops*; it was always a total pleasure. We were treated well by everyone, and the drinks would flow after the show at the legendary BBC bar! We certainly stood out – eight blokes in teddy boy outfits. But the great thing was that you would mingle with everyone: the Police were fans of ours as it happens, and we would often sink a few with Sting and company. But that was the *Pops*, it was a family! We would go up in the lift with the Boomtown Rats and have a natter... Cliff, Metallica, you name it, we may have been doing different music – but we were all in it together!

"I recall doing 'You Got What It Takes' live, and my drainpipes were so tight that when I knelt down – I heard a *rip,* and the crown jewels popped out on display! I quickly stood to the side and sort of covered up as best I could, much to the delight of the crew and production staff!

"We were the 'wind-up' merchants... always trying it on. I once told Les Gray from Mud that we were going to walk onto the stage with a donkey, just to see if they would try and top it!"

David Essex was another who could never contain his exuberant delight when he made an appearance on the show. But for the amiable Essex, it could all have been so very different. After years in the pop wilderness, it all happened at once: *Godspell,* 'Rock On', *That'll Be the Day...* "I remember my first appearance on the show in 1973, and I was planning to wear a sleeveless black T-shirt and black jeans for 'Rock On'. But after rehearsal, the producer Robin Nash stormed to the stage saying: 'You will disappear darling. Wear something white!' Now that threw the record company into a panic, and someone had to shoot out to get hold of a cream suit, which ironically then, of course, became the 'look' for early Essex!"

Another act who was quite deliberate about his early 70s look was Gilbert O'Sullivan: "The Beatles didn't need to have collarless suits or Beatle haircuts, but they did – and that made a huge impression on me. So what was I going to do? I wanted to look different... and my love of Chaplin and Buster Keaton led to the bob-tail jacket – which I hired from Berman's, the theatrical costumiers, and the Just William tie... So I really created the character of 'Gilbert'. I felt that sitting at the piano you were restricted, so the clothes gave people something to look at. That was a light thing, it wasn't serious, but what I *was* serious about was the music. I was not stupid, I knew I was a good songwriter, the record companies and publishers liked my songs, but they all wanted me to look 'normal': put a pair of jeans on, grow your hair… And there's no doubt I would have sold far more records looking like James Taylor!"

Amidst the blue jean boogie of Status Quo and the glittering excess of Slade, the programme always welcomed the slick soul sound of the Stylistics. But *looking* at the group, you are struck now by how much they resemble a quintet of steak-house waiters. And then there were the Jacksons!

In 1972 thirteen-year-old Michael Jackson made his *TOTP* debut alongside his brothers in the Jackson 5, with 'Looking Through the Window'. Ann Mann, who was working on the programme in the 1970s, recalled "being stopped by a lost and vulnerable little boy called Michael Jackson in TV Centre reception, and escorting him back to his brothers in the Green Assembly room".

Five years later, on the eve of *Off the Wall*, Michael led his siblings through 'Show You the Way to Go.' You cannot fault the performance – and the poignancy of seeing the proudly African-American Michael exultant and in control… But what *were* they wearing? The brothers were clad in what looked like uniforms filched from the Ruritanian Royal Protection Squad.

One act who developed a unique relationship with the programme over the years as a songwriter and performer, was Manchester-born Graham Gouldman. Graham's association with *Top of the Pops* began even before the show was broadcast: "I was part of the warm-up band in the original Manchester church, we were called the Mockingbirds. I had already written hits for the Hollies and Herman's Hermits, but I had a very odd experience when one of the first bands on the show was the Yardbirds with 'For Your Love', a song I had actually written! That was a very weird show for me.

"Our first time on as 10cc was in 1972 with 'Donna', and we were amidst all that glittered, fashion-wise. So when we walked on in our denims and jeans, Tony Blackburn walked up to us and said 'Hey guys… great gimmick!'

"In 1980, I had a solo single – 'Sunburn' – and it was doing okay in the charts. We did a pre-record, and were very excited because an appearance on *Top of the Pops* almost guaranteed a hit. We were waiting for the show to go out, but then the Wimbledon coverage ran over, and the show never saw the light of day. I was devastated. No *Pops*… no hit!"

What would now be called 'audience reach' really registered with the programme during its glory days of the 1970s, as Linda Lewis recalled: "The first time I was on in 1973, I couldn't believe it! I was more like a fan, even though 'Rock A-Doodle Do' was a hit. I was in love with Kid Jensen and I remember asking Michael Jackson for his autograph – who I remember as a shy, sweet little black boy. Later on, I mostly remember mucking about in the BBC bar with Mud, Hot Chocolate and David Essex (who I also had a crush on). Oh yeah, and having to change my lyrics to 'Rock & Roller Coaster' as they were considered too saucy… In fact, as far as *TOTP* goes, the BBC bar features heavily in my memory!"

Strangely, one of the 1970s' best-known hits came from one of its lesser-known acts. Released as the first single from the Tim Rice & Andrew Lloyd Webber musical *Evita* (the original album of which also featured David Essex, as Che Guevara), 'Don't Cry For Me Argentina' was sung on disc by actress Julie Covington. But Julie declined the role on stage and, while the single reigned, refused to appear to promote it. Which meant that whenever 'Don't Cry For Me Argentina' was featured on *Top of the Pops* it was either danced to, or played over a montage of images of the real Eva Peron. But despite all that, Julie Covington remains part of an elite group: one of only four British female artists to have sold a million plus copies of a single in the UK (along with Leona Lewis, Alexandra Burke and Adele).

Beginning back in the 1960s with Amen Corner, Andy Fairweather-Low went on to enjoy a glittering career, playing with Eric Clapton, the Who, Roger Waters and George Harrison – as he confirmed when reminiscing about *Top of the Pops*: "I never started out to be a singer – I was, and still am, a guitarist at heart. From the Amen Corner days right through to Fairweather and my solo career, I always felt a bit difficult being up there in the front. It was indeed a necessary evil. I was not a natural singer, but I recall being on the show with Fairweather when 'Natural Sinner' was a hit – with dreadful hair and big boots… I looked a right mess! I was an appalling mimer too! I was on the show once, with 'Reggae Tune' in the mid-70s, and my manager Chris Williams overheard someone in the control room mutter as he looked at me on stage: 'He could get a job in a crime drama – as a dead body…'"

By the mid-70s, *Top of the Pops* had become a national institution, with approximately 25% of the UK population diligently watching every Thursday evening. No wonder then, that in 1974 the BBC launched the perfect Christmas present: *The Top of the Pops Annual*, which was published for the next 10 years.

The fact that the show was broadcast weekly for such a long period of time meant that while the acts came and went, the presenters remained constant favourites. Culled from the nation's only national pop radio network, the Radio 1 DJs were soon as popular as the artists they introduced. With listening figures running into millions, Tony Blackburn, Noel Edmonds, Dave Lee Travis and David Hamilton became household names, mobbed whenever they opened a supermarket or appeared at a discotheque.

Dave Lee Travis first presented the show in November 1973, replacing Kenny Everett who had defected to the recently-launched Capital Radio. DLT remembers worrying the production crew when he wanted to ride in on a motor bike to introduce Chris Spedding's hit 'Motorbikin': "All I wanted to do was pop in on a little 50cc bike," he told Shaun Tilley, "but they thought I meant 500cc!... Years ago I made inquiries about seeing a tape of my first appearance, but the BBC response was that it had been wiped and had a *Gardeners' World* taped over it!"

"In June 1973 I was given my own daily show on Radio 1," David Hamilton recalled. "Noel Edmonds on breakfast, Tony Blackburn in the morning, Johnnie Walker at lunchtime, and me in the afternoon... In 1973 there were only two music stations in the UK, Radio 1 and Radio 2, but all that was about to change. Britain's first commercial stations, Capital and LBC, were about to launch in London in October... Our job was to try to hold on to the enormous audience Radio 1 had enjoyed for 6 glorious years.

"I made my first appearance on *Top of the Pops* on 22 January 1976. The first thing that struck me was how small the studio was. With clever direction it appeared much bigger, but in fact, no more than a hundred teenagers were hustled from set to set. I never knew quite what to wear. Once I bought a white suit I was rather proud of. Introducing cool dude and fashion icon Bryan Ferry singing 'Let's Stick Together', I noticed he was wearing a white suit too, so I said that we looked like 'two ice cream salesmen'. Bryan was not amused!

"In those days the BBC really didn't pay much money. My fee never rose above £100. We recorded the shows on a Wednesday night, and after the recording I used to dash off to do a disco in a pub in the Old Kent Road, where I got paid around £400. It amazed me that a national show watched by millions paid so little compared to a pub with an audience of 200 – but, of course,

Top of the Pops provided the shop window that led to the gigs.

"To understand the appeal of *Top of the Pops* in the 70s, one has to remember that pop music appealed to all age groups. Artists like David Cassidy and the Osmonds were adored as much by grandparents as grandchildren, and entire families sat around the television set to see what was in the charts that week. With no music channels, it was *the* big visual outlet for the stars of the day.

"In 1977 my picture on the set of *Top of the Pops* appeared on the cover of the *Sunday Telegraph* magazine with the caption: 'David Hamilton – Housewives' Superstar'. My flared trousers handily covered my four-inch platform shoes and for the first time in my life I looked tall!

"By the end of 1977... I moved to Radio 2, thus ending my days on *Top of the Pops* which definitely didn't use Radio 2 DJs! I did appear again on the 25th anniversary edition when there was an enormous off-set spat between Simon Bates and Tony Blackburn and I almost had to drag them apart... the happy sound of Radio 1!

"The show was an institution and I'm so glad I did it. As the singles chart became less important, its significance dwindled but I'm sure it could have lived on as an album chart show. Unfortunately, the BBC didn't keep all the editions, but back in the 70s I had a home video recorder and when I moved home a while ago I found some recordings in a cupboard under the stairs – which may be the only remaining copies of some shows. The quality is almost as good as an original recording."

∗ ∗ ∗

Unfortunately, all too often the vacuity of the *Top of the Pops* DJs' appearances left them wide open to criticism – and eventually parody. Because the content of the show was based on popular opinion – if enough people bought a record, it eventually made its way onto *Top of the Pops* – there was really no reason for DLT or 'Diddy' David to analyse or critique the records they were introducing. But the sheer persistent jolliness of the jocks, particularly during the programme's glory days, is still capable of making one squirm. Cynics felt it was like being trapped in a lift with an unremittingly jolly Redcoat.

It was to those chirpy Radio 1 DJs that Harry Enfield and Paul Whitehouse turned in the 1990s, for their sketches as that pop-tastically painful pair, Smashie & Nicey. Their spot-on skewering of that particularly vacuous *TOTP*-type of DJ insincerity coincided with a new broom at Radio 1, effectively kebabbing the old-school disc jockeying for ever. But actually, old DJs never die; they just slip away, to local radio...

Watching some of the vintage episodes again, you are reminded of how great *Top of the Pops* looked: even on a small 1970s television set, the scale seemed enormous. Cavernous sets; sweeping camera movements; tracking shots through energetically dancing crowds; the bright lights... the logo... the stars! But if you concentrate hard, it appears that whichever act was performing, the audience is locked into that same curious *Top of the Pops* dance – well, dance is probably stretching it... It was more a *TOTP* Shuffle really, and it was always the same. Whether Boney M, Baccara or Bob Marley was playing, the audience would stand on the same spot, necking the monitor and occasionally undertaking a strange below-waist, treading-grape action, while their upper body appeared to be attempting to balance a parrot on each shoulder.

Paul Burnett was another Radio 1 jock who soon graduated to the show: "My first time on the show was with Tony Blackburn in 1974. It was all so new, and as we sat in his dressing room he turned to me and said 'Do you know what that smell is? 'No' I said... '*Fear*' he replied with a glint in his eye! Robin Nash had a few tips for me: 'Why not wear a bow-tie dear boy... and smile a bit more.' Well that was really Robin encapsulated, the smiling, bow-tied gent... However, I really didn't think that was quite the right look for the Disco era, though I did find a use for the bow-tie he gave me... rolled up and stuffed down my Bee Gees-style tight white trousers!

"As one half of Laurie Lingo & the Dipsticks with DLT, we had our taste of life on the other side, when our 'Convoy GB' single made the Top Ten in the spring of 1976. We were at No. 4 when we went on the show, Dave as 'Super Scouse' dressed in a Superman type costume, and me as 'Plastic Chicken' dressed as, you guessed it, a chicken! In rehearsal, to disguise the fact that he kept forgetting the words, Dave accused me of trying to 'crack him up' much to the annoyance of the floor manager. I can still see that floor manager's red face screaming at me through the hole in my beak! Needless to say our *TOTP* appearance was not a great success and, not surprisingly, after a couple of weeks the record was out of the charts altogether! Still, it had given us a taste of what the show could mean for an artist and of course the power it had over the record buying public – especially the discerning ones!"

* * *

The arrival of Punk in 1976–77 posed a very different sort of problem for *TOTP*. The whole ethos of the new music was 'Us versus Them'; the kids against The Man; and anything that suggested compromise, or cosying up to the Establishment, reeked of betrayal. It has to be said that there was something exciting, inspiring – even revolutionary – in the air during those first gobby days of punk rock. Over the decades since rock & roll first burst onto the scene, the music industry had grown remote, complacent and out of touch; but there was a real incendiary energy to the UK punk scene – and it sent a tremor through the whole music business.

For the first time since its 60s heyday, rock & roll witnessed a new movement, one which it had not sanctioned. Suddenly the 'old farts' weren't the Rolling Stones and Yes, they were *us*.

Producer Robin Nash was one of those in the firing line during that tremulous punk period: "I certainly went through a difficult period in those times," he admitted to Steve Blacknell. "There was a lot of heart-searching that used to go on, because in consideration of your show and your audience, you never wanted to destroy the level of artistic creativity. Mind you, I did take exception when a certain member of a group turned up wearing a jacket with a certain four-letter word on the back… There was no way I could stand for that!"

By April 1977, singles by the Sex Pistols, the Stranglers and the Clash had all registered on the charts. But it was the Jam – with their first single, 'In the City' – who became the first punk group to appear on *Top of the Pops*. Pop obsessive Paul Weller claims that one of his first-ever memories was seeing the Small Faces on the programme, and he certainly wasn't afraid of denting his punk credibility by appearing on *Top of the Pops*.

The Punk threat didn't actually last long, and in terms of sales, punk was a mere blip. None of which denies the Sex Pistols' significance as the most influential British band since the Beatles.

In terms of impact and influence the Pistols made many disciples; but they sold comparatively few records. So it was inevitable that while eschewing the programme (and being shunned by the musical establishment) the Sex Pistols eventually relented, and in July 1977 allowed a video of them performing their third single, 'Pretty Vacant', to be broadcast on *TOTP*. In 1996, the band did finally appear in person on *Top of the Pops*, performing live – to help promote their aptly-named Filthy Lucre tour.

After the Pistols, the Clash were the best-remembered and most-respected of all the punk bands. But they always boycotted the show believing that miming to a pre-recorded backing track would undermine their punk credibility. In the event, the Clash's debut single 'White Riot' only reached No.38 – without doubt, a *TOTP* appearance would have seen it rise much higher.

Tony Parsons admitted to Marcus Gray: "I can see now that there were masses of contradictions in punk. We were all part of the music business. [the Clash] were on CBS, and I was writing for an IPC magazine. It was all mixed up…"

Ironically, the Clash's 1982 single 'Should I Stay or Should I Go' was later used as part of the inexorable TV advertising campaign for Levi jeans, giving the band a No.1 hit in 1991 – but by then the band were long gone. Joe Strummer broke his *TOTP* embargo in June 1996, when he appeared on the programme – alongside Lily Allen's dad Keith – in Black Grape performing their No.1 single, the Euro '96 anthem 'England's Irie'.

Legend has it that chart-friendly punks the Stranglers were hailed by *NME*'s Charles Shaar Murray, who reckoned that if the Stranglers ever appeared on *Top Of the Pops* they'd destroy the studio. In fact, on their first appearance in 1977, the band brought along brushes and brooms and gave their dressing room a good old tidy! Amazingly, the original line-up made 13 *TOTP* appearances between 1977 and 1990 – when founder member Hugh Cornwell left. And surely, they remain the only act ever to name-check both Lenin and Trotsky on *Top of the Pops*?

The Boomtown Rats, the Jam, the Damned, Sham 69, X-Ray Specs, the Adverts, the Buzzcocks and Jilted John were just some of the punk acts who graced *Top of the Pops* during the late 70s. As, of course, did the Rezillos with their Top Twenty hit 'Top of the Pops'.

Of course, the Jam were much more than simply a punk phenomenon. In chart terms, they equalled Slade's success in the 1970s – being the first group since the Brummie quartet to have three singles enter the charts at No. 1.

Right: Simon & Garfunkel in the UK for a rare Top of the Pops *appearance in June 1966*

Even now, you can see that keening, frantic energy coming off the trio when you watch them plugging 'In the City' on their *TOTP* debut. Learning that they were No.1 for the first time with 'Going Underground', the Jam curtailed their first (and only) American tour to fly home and appear on *Top of the Pops*. And for one particular *Pops* performance of the song in April 1980, for reasons best known to himself, Paul Weller appeared wearing an apron.

Ironically it was in 1982, on the eve of their split, that the Jam celebrated their third No.1 – the double A-sided 'Town Called Malice' and 'Precious' – becoming the first group since Paul Weller's faves, the Beatles, to perform *both* sides of their No.1 on the programme.

Bass player Bruce Foxton recalled the band's swansong: "It was the last time we appeared as the Jam. It was for 'The Bitterest Pill', and I had a really bad cold at the time. I had been taking a nightly cold cure medicine, unfortunately the record company people kept on buying round after round of drinks in the bar, and I ended up being a little 'worse for wear'… When I watched my performance back on the video a little later I looked like something resembling a stuffed owl!"

One of the most committed and tenacious of all the punk groups were the UK Subs, much beloved by the late and much-missed Carol Clerk of *Melody Maker*. Bassist and occasional producer John McCoy confessed: "No one was more surprised than me to have a string of hits with the UK Subs. When they were asked on the show, at the time, vocals were done live. There was a last minute panic as we were to go to air – the song was 'Tomorrow's Girls' and it had one line 'Tomorrow's girls are gonna piss it in your ear…', which had all the BBC production staff, the band's management, and myself, all trying to persuade singer Charlie Harper to change it. Of course, he milked the situation right up until the very start of the song… and then, at literally the last moment, changed the line to 'stick it in your ear!' Very silly stuff…

"Another occasion that springs to mind was when I appeared with John Du Cann on his hit 'Don't Be A Dummy'. This was in fact Johnny Du Cann, who had this hard rock image with Hard Stuff, Bullet, and he was concerned about this hit damaging his image as guitarist from Atomic Rooster! I got John some courage – which was not Dutch, if you see what I mean – and we literally flew through the *TOTP* appearance, giggling the whole time… Can't remember who else was in the band. In fact, can't remember anything much else about that appearance!"

* * *

Squeeze – whose built-in tunesmith team, Difford & Tilbrook, tapped into a rich vein of Englishness, very much in the style of Ray Davies – enjoyed an unforgettable run of distinctive hits during the late 70s and early 80s. The band's Chris Difford had few doubts about the basis of the show's appeal: "It is the essential programme to be on, the Heinz of pop music: 57 varieties of acts, and all different. Variety – that was the key."

Another band who comfortably outlasted their punk contemporaries were the Police, but their real success came in the 1980s, so let's wait a while for them…

New York's Blondie also managed to survive and transcended punk, with a career that stretched way beyond the 1970s; and being blessed with charismatic singer Debbie Harry, they were always a televisual treat. Blondie were feted on *Top of the Pops* when 'Heart Of Glass' and 'Sunday Girl' both reached No.1 during 1979. And they topped that the following year with 'Atomic', 'Call Me' and 'The Tide is High' – giving them three further chart-toppers within the calendar year.

Blessed with supermodel looks and cheekbones that looked like they were sculpted, Debbie Harry was a cameraman's dream. But Blondie were always more than just their singer, and their run of beguiling pop singles ensures that a Blondie *Best Of…* really merits the title. A run of 13 UK Top Ten hits (including those previously mentioned No. 1s) made Blondie the most successful American group of the period. Incredibly, that run of success was extended 20 years later, when 'Maria' gave Blondie a 1999 No. 1. And then in 2013, long after the demise of the *Pops*, One Direction reached No.1 with the Blondie cover 'One Way Or Another'.

Punk may have sent shockwaves through the musical establishment, but in certain circles it wasn't welcomed with open arms: "Punk rock? I tried to block it out of my mind," Tony Blackburn told Jeff Simpson. "I hated punk and the punk era. It was horrible."

Undeniably though, the punk groups who did appear on the show were all there in response to what the record-buying public wanted. As ever, the essence of *Top of the Pops* was that it reflected the charts, and if punk groups were represented in the charts, then they merited a place on the *Pops*. One memorably eclectic programme of 1978 found the Buzzcocks and Jam appearing alongside Brotherhood of Man and Leo Sayer.

Oh, and while we're on Brotherhood of Man… it is only on re-viewing their appearances that one appreciates just how 'Abba-lite' the quartet were. I mean, have you *heard* 'Angelo' recently? And then played Abba's 'Fernando'? But the mum and dad friendly Brotherhood… obviously tapped into a very popular vein, chalking up 21 *TOTP* appearances between 1970 and 1982.

In December 1977, Elton John scored a first when he became the first non-DJ to present the programme. Elton was already one of the biggest stars of the decade – and at one point it was estimated that 2% of all records being sold around the world were by the artist formerly known as Reg Dwight! But although by then a National Treasure (Royal Variety show; Morecambe & Wise Christmas guest), according to Jeff Simpson, Elton only made a paltry handful of appearances on *Top of the Pops* during his heyday in the 1970s: once as presenter; once accompanying T. Rex on 'Get It On'; and just three times in his own right. Mind you, it famously also took Elton a staggering 20 years to attain his first solo UK No.1 single.

Another gentle irony came in 1977, with one of the most memorable *Top of the Pops* appearances of all time. As punk roared and raged all around, and disco strutted its stuff, a true legend made his only live appearance on the programme. Bing Crosby, who had been next door at the BBC recording an appearance on Michael Parkinson's chat show, literally popped into the *Pops* studio to croon 'That's What Life is All About'. As the singer of 'White Christmas' (at that time the biggest-selling single ever), Bing was made warmly welcome.

Producer Stan Appel noticed former Prime Minister Edward Heath in the gallery watching the legend at work: "The word had obviously got round TV Centre, because the studio that evening was filled with people all eagerly waiting to see him. Bing walked into the studio and everyone, and I mean everyone, just stood up and applauded quite spontaneously."

***

In terms of celebrity, Paul McCartney continued to pack a punch during his post-Beatles career. Seven years on since the Fab Four split, Paul's group Wings ("the group the Beatles could have become" in the expert opinion of Alan Partridge) scored their only UK No.1 with 'Mull Of Kintyre'. The lilting Scottish lament arrived at the very toppermost of the poppermost during the first week of December 1977, and stayed there for an incredible 9 weeks. So while 1977 may now be remembered as the year of the Punk/Disco see-saw, it is worth reflecting that it was also the year when 'Mull Of Kintyre' became the first single *ever* to sell more than 2 million copies in the UK.

As was his habit, McCartney would regularly check in with his London office about current record sales – but even he was surprised to learn that his current single was shifting 145,000 copies a day! On its way into the record books, 'Mull Of Kintyre' even beat the UK's previous best-selling single – a little number that Paul also had a hand in: 'She Loves You' by the Beatles.

The 'Mull of Kintyre' video, seen regularly on *Top of the Pops*, memorably featured the Campbeltown Pipe Band – primed with copious tins of McEwan's Export, courtesy of local resident Mr P. McCartney. And few will forget the sight of Wings accompanied by the Pipe Band on that year's Christmas edition.

One act who seemed effortlessly to escape the wrath of the punks was David Bowie. Fascinating now, to watch that epochal 'Starman' from 1972 and then leap 5 years (how very David Bowie) to see him performing 'Heroes' on the show in 1977. By then, Ziggy, Aladdin and the Thin White Duke had been consigned to the dustbin of Bowie history. Here instead, was David in civvies: a blue jean baby, casual and charismatic, strolling through one of his greatest songs. He really should have brushed his hair though…

It wasn't just the space cadets who came in Bowie's wake, he had fans at every level. Peter Powell, who joined Radio 1 as a DJ in 1977, admitted: "My all-time hero, now and forever, was David Bowie; and only once in 10 years did I get the chance to introduce him on the show… It was November 1977, and I was totally star struck and virtually lost for words as to how to introduce him, he performed like a mega-God and yes, very aptly, it was 'Heroes'! And for the first and *only* time in my entire *TOTP* career, did a star guest knock on my dressing room door to say thank you – and yes, it was David Bowie! There really is a God…

"Over 10 years on the show you naturally build a great camaraderie with the production team, and when I left they very kindly threw a leaving party. In a book they put together, of my worst moments, there was a stark reminder of my first show, as a very young inexperienced presenter. There I was, a bag of nerves, standing awaiting the countdown to go live – on *Top of the Pops*! My heart was in my mouth, and with just 30 seconds to go, the floor manager whispered in my ear that my flies were undone... Total panic and a look that would do justice to any horror movie – but the nerves were gone in an instant!

"And of course they were not undone, but it did the trick: the show went live and I lived to get rebooked. I once even had the honour of introducing a one-hit wonder by someone dressed up as a dog... and a few years later it was revealed that inside the dog costume was the one and only Simon Cowell!"

✳ ✳ ✳

Elvis Costello and the Attractions made a number of memorable appearances on the show during the late 70s when they enjoyed a run of classic pop 45s. Although Elvis's first appearance, to promote his third single 'Red Shoes', was one of those rare occasions when a *TOTP* performance didn't register with record buyers and the single failed to chart – perhaps because it was broadcast barely a fortnight after the death of 'the other Elvis'.

However, Costello went on to make some blistering *TOTP* appearances throughout the 70s – 'Watching the Detectives', '(I Don't Want To Go To) Chelsea', 'Pump It Up', 'Radio Radio', 'Oliver's Army'... And though he remains one of the era's more unlikely looking idols – with his Buddy Holly glasses and gap-toothed sneer – few performers have ever matched Costello's intensity.

'Hate and revenge,' Costello had claimed as his motivations for writing in one of his earliest print interviews. Yet there he was, happily miming along on *Top of the Pops* in an effort to reach out into the living rooms of the nation. But then everyone recognised the huge power the programme exerted on the UK music business; artists cancelled holidays, chartered jets, and switched concerts around just so they could appear on the show.

Costello's Stiff label-mate Ian Dury also made a number of well-remembered *TOTP* appearances, particularly when it came to 'Hit Me With Your Rhythm Stick'. Besides providing Stiff with its first No. 1, Dury and the Blockheads commemorated the occasion in January 1979 by appearing in dinner suits.

It was no coincidence that the 1970s saw the largest ever audiences for *Top of the Pops*, with weekly viewing figures around the 15 million mark – and an 18 month waiting list to become a member of the jiving studio audience. It was in 1979 – in the aftermath of glam, but with disco full steam ahead – that sales of UK singles reached an all-time high, with 89 million going across the counter in one year.

Further evidence – just in case you *still* doubt the awesome power of the programme – comes from Roxy Music's drummer, Paul Thompson who went to see a friend play at a Newcastle club, but didn't have a membership card. He was anticipating trouble getting in, until the doorman commented: "It's all right son, you can go in. I saw you on *Top of the Pops*."

* * *

One key *Top of the Pops* edition in 1979 was a futuristic programme, boasting Roxy Music; Bowie's video for 'Boys Keep Swinging'; and natural heir, Gary Numan, making his *TOTP* debut with 'Are Friends Electric?' "I grew up with *Top of the Pops*," Gary recalled. "To me, as a young boy, it was the pinnacle of success. If you were on *Top of the Pops* you had made it to the very top. I still thought that the week before I first went on it, as a complete unknown.

"I was very lucky. The record company decided to take a huge risk and print 20,000 copies of my fourth single, 'Are Friends Electric', as a picture disc. It was a huge risk because my biggest seller so far had only sold 3,000 copies in total. And 'Are Friends Electric' wasn't picking up any radio play, the song was way too long for a pop single, you couldn't dance to it, *and* it had no vocal chorus! But those 20,000 picture discs sold quickly and turned it into an instant collector's item, selling to people who had never even heard the song!

"At that time *TOTP* had a weekly spot called 'Bubbling Under', where they would play a song that wasn't high in the chart, but which was showing reasonable movement at the low end... I'm told it was between me and Simple Minds that particular week – and they chose me because they thought my band, Tubeway Army, had a more interesting sounding name.

"Being asked to appear was a dream come true, and a nightmare, all rolled into one! Even being in the same BBC building as so many of my heroes had been before was amazing. But to walk into the *TOTP* studio was something else entirely – and if my career had ended right there it would have been enough. I had got on *Top of the Pops*! The nightmare part of it was knowing just how enormous and life-changing an opportunity it was, and not wanting to mess it up... A good *TOTP* performance and you could look forward to an entirely new life. A bad one, and you could find yourself lost and forgotten for ever more. It really was that powerful.

"I remember thinking the BBC crew, who had surely seen every great act in the world, would be arrogant, rude and unhelpful, but they were anything but.

Bearing in mind that I was yet to have any success, I was the unknown outsider on his first appearance with no hit single in the chart, they couldn't have been more helpful. I asked for all the coloured light gels to be taken out as I just wanted white light. I asked for some of the lights to be positioned low so that shadows would fall up my face. I asked for all kinds of things and they were only too happy to change their set up to give me what I wanted. I wanted to make sure we stood out and changing the lighting was an important part of that, as *TOTP* did tend to have a generic look that everyone lived with. I thought they would be reluctant to change that look, but they seemed excited that someone was actually taking that level of interest.

"Thank goodness, it went well for me. 'Are Friends Electric' went to No. 1 and stayed there for a month. I went back on *Top of the Pops* many times after that and always enjoyed it... In my opinion it remains the most influential TV show for music that the UK has ever had and I'm proud to have been involved with it – and the great people behind it – along the way."

Another equally striking *Top of the Pops* debut also occurred near the end of that decade. Kate Bush's 1978 No. 1 'Wuthering Heights' divides opinion to this day: for some, it is the apogee of unique, haunted femininity; for others, the banshee wail grates like fingers dragged across a blackboard. Whatever, the song was by the first female artist to have entirely written her own No. 1. But given that Kate Bush only ever undertook a single concert tour, and her personal appearances were limited to a handful, her *Top of the Pops* appearances have inevitably become cherished.

Kate Bush told Steve Blacknell about making her *Top of the Pops* debut while still in her teens: "It was my first ever television show in the UK, so you can imagine how I felt. Let's just say that I was more than a little nervous... But whatever the nerves and tension are like on the night, it is still always worth doing the show, whatever it takes. Because I think, as do a lot of other artists, that it is still one of the most important shows for promoting a single."

* * *

Now, can you name the only group to have two singles in the UK's Top Ten biggest sellers of all time? That would be the Beatles then? Nope, actually it was a 1970s quartet called... Boney M! The multi-racial group had been put together by German music executive Frank Farian, who fashioned both 'Rivers Of Babylon/Brown Girl In the Ring' and 'Mary's Boy Child/Oh My Lord' – their multi-million sellers of 1978.

For much of the rest of 1978 *Top of the Pops* might as well have been re-named *Grease*, after the film musical that harked back to a fantasy version of the 1950s, and produced the mega-hits 'You're the One That I Want' and 'Summer Nights'. Sadly, such was the stature of the two stars – John Travolta and Olivia Newton-John – that *TOTP* had to make do with clips of them singing taken from the movie. Again and again and again... throughout 1978.

Left: *The Who backstage at* Top of the Pops *in Manchester, promoting their first hit, 'I Can't Explain'*

"The worst thing I ever saw on *TOTP*," Tony Blackburn told Ian Gittins, "was 'You're the One That I Want' by Hylda Baker and Arthur Mullard! It was horrible." But such was the momentum behind *Grease* at the time, that even that truly 'horrible' novelty single reached No. 22 in the chart.

Symbolically, when the Boomtown Rats' song 'Rat Trap' deposed 'Summer Nights', singer Bob Geldof (looking and acting uncannily like Mick Jagger) tore up a picture of John Travolta live on air! Horror! Shock! But both Geldof and Travolta survived the incident.

But Geldof was nevertheless pragmatic about the programme: "*Top of the Pops* was the single most important pop show in the country," he wrote in his autobiography. "We knew that an appearance could make the difference between failure and success for a record. In the New Wave gestalt, as defined by *New Musical Express*, the fashionable view of … *Top of the Pops* was that it was part of the decadent old order which had to be overthrown… By going on *Top of the Pops* we were supposedly betraying the values of the New Wave and were in danger of being smeared by that most awful of accusations, commercialism. I had no time for this sort of nonsense… I wanted to sell records. I wanted as many people to see us as possible."

That all round good-egg, Nick Lowe, had also sneaked in on the coat-tails of the New Wave. And one of the abiding images of 1978 is a photo of him, on the *Pops* to promote his only hit 'I Love the Sound of Breaking Glass'. Resplendent in his lurid green suit, styled on that of Batman's Riddler, Nick's hands are forming a triangle as he formulates his theories of 'pure pop for now people' to a grinning and visibly delighted Andy Williams…

Just try to imagine what it was like back in 1978: you have hot-footed in from school, or that first dead-end job, and settled down in front of the TV set one night in 1978. You jostle for space with sisters keen to gasp over their teen idols, while you want a slice of the new punk action. Dad, lighting up his first fag after a fried tea, is looking forward to ogling Pan's People, while mum hopes that one of those *nice* singers like Des O'Connor or Dana will be on that night.

But if the parents are otherwise occupied and you have the technology, you'll huddle up close to the family's only TV set with a cassette player to record your favourites so that you can play them back endlessly – blissfully unaware that home taping is killing music.

Here was a rare opportunity to see the acts which *NME* and, belatedly,

Melody Maker and *Sounds* had been writing about from their exalted locations in London. It was a year that saw Terry Wogan juxtaposed with (ex-Sex Pistol) Glenn Matlock's Rich Kids; guitar-whiz Gordon Giltrap; and Bob Marley – all on one show. Which saw Plastic Bertrand – the man *NME* dubbed "the sound of angry young Belgium", strutting his Gallic punk stuff. And here too were the Smurfs – appearing alongside those eager young men from C&A, the Undertones.

Other memorable *Top of the Pops* backstage encounters included the Wurzels and Bob Marley; Cliff Richard and the Who; the Human League and Bucks Fizz; the Damned and Elkie Brooks; the Wedding Present and Jason Donovan; Slade and… well, pretty well everybody: "We'd get pissed with Mud or Status Quo," Noddy Holder told Ian Gittins. "We took the Osmonds to Tramp on their first visit. But the band who were really as mad as fucking hatters were Boney M!" Meanwhile dancer Sue Menhenick was chatting to Motorhead's Lemmy, who she remembered as always being "polite and charming!"

Fondly remembered as hippie stoners, Dr Hook & the Medicine Show had enjoyed an enduring 1972 hit with 'Sylvia's Mother', and the same year produced that ultra-rare single 'Cover of the *Radio Times*'. But by the late 70s they had been reborn as Dr Hook, on a new label, which led to a run of hits. Singer Dennis Locorriere remembered: "'More Like the Movies' was hovering just outside the Top 40… and EMI were pretty sure that when the midweeks were released we would be in the 40, and therefore would qualify to be on the show. So, it's hard to believe now, but they flew us over on Concorde! They put us in a hotel where we would just sit and wait and see what happened. I had a cracked rib at the time… but such was the power of the *Pops*, that nothing else mattered.

"Sure enough, we made the 40 and appeared on the show alongside a young Kate Bush. I sang 'live' and although the high notes sure hurt my chest I sang through the pain! But it was worth it – we got to No. 14! And next year, 'When You're In Love With A Beautiful Woman' made it to No. 1 – so we really *were* Top of the Pops!

"However much pain I was in, it was always worth it to appear on the show… It helped our career no end – and it was always a thrill."

In 1979, during one of the many 'folk revivals', Fiddler's Dram enjoyed a singalong hit with 'Day Trip To Bangor', unsettling *TOTP* dancers who were more used to energetic disco breaks than Morris dancing. While the group looked delighted, if rather baffled by their appearance, they laid the foundations for one of the outfits who did go on to lead the folk revival in later years – the Oyster Band.

Also making his *TOTP* debut that year was Radio 1's Andy Peebles, who had just taken over the afternoon show from Tony Blackburn. At the time, Blackburn had been using his show to mourn the break-up of his marriage to Tessa Wyatt. "I remember lying in my bath shouting at the radio: 'Tony, stop it, shut up!'" Peebles told Shaun Tilley. "On the *Pops*, you were given the opportunity to meet your idols, people you had worshipped from afar – and that sometimes turned out to be bitterly disappointing, or better than you had ever dreamt! On occasion, you had to introduce people for whom you had absolutely no time at all for, in musical terms!"

With radio his preferred medium, Peebles had been reluctant to appear on the show, and it was to be a further 2 years before he presented another *TOTP*. "Well that would send the message that they tried me out and didn't think me good enough... I think there were other people around at the time – Peter Powell was very, *very* good at hosting the show, he looked great, terrific smile, very enthusiastic..."

As the decade crept to its close, it seemed beyond ironic that the final UK No.1 single of the 1970s came from a band releasing their first single in 11 years, who had made a point of *not* appearing on the programme to promote it. Yes, it was Pink Floyd's 'Another Brick in the Wall (Part 2)'. Given the band's reluctance to emerge from behind their mysterious Wall, the single's success was buoyed by Gerald Scarfe's disturbing video.

So after all the musical changes that extraordinary decade had witnessed: from glam, through punk, and disco... By 1979 you couldn't help but agree with UK music mogul Mickie Most, who worked with everyone from Donovan to Jeff Beck and Lulu to Suzi Quatro: "If you don't get on the show – you're kippered!"

CHAPTER 3
The 1980s:
Don't Look Back in Anger

A star back in the 1960s... The figure who dominated the 1970s... But just how would David Bowie cope with the new decade? Very well, thank you for asking; and largely thanks to the new-fangled format of the promotional video.

Bowie's first hit of the new decade came with 'Ashes to Ashes' in August 1980, which found the former David Jones revisiting his old 'Space Oddity' chum Major Tom. Coincidentally, it was also his first No.1 since a re-released 'Space Oddity' back in 1975.

This 1980s rebirth coincided with Bowie's stage appearance on Broadway, starring in *The Elephant Man*. He was, incidentally, very good indeed – I was in town on an assignment for *Melody Maker* and was lucky enough to catch a performance. Bowie was spellbinding as John Merrick, no make-up, just a spellbinding stage presence.

But his absence from the UK meant that *Top of the Pops* had to rely on the song's video. Bowie was dressed as Pierrot in the promo, strolling along Hastings beach, surrounded by hand-picked New Romantic extras from the uber-trendy Blitz Club. One figure notable for his absence was Bowie-obsessive Boy George; he would have to wait a couple more years for his *Top of the Pops* debut, this time in his own right.

Sadly though, it was not the Culture Club singer's performance that caused the BBC switchboard to become jammed when he first appeared on the show in 1982, to promote 'Do You Really Want To Hurt Me'; it was complaints and enquiries about Boy George's sexual identity. Quoted in 2012's *The Million Sellers*, Boy George said: "All the artists I had loved had been on *TOTP* – Bowie, Marc Bolan, Roxy Music..." Remembering the time when his own single was quite low in the charts he explained: "We got on there by default... back then

LEFT: Morrissey leads the Smiths on a 1989 Top of the Pops *appearance*

records could bubble under for some time before climbing. I think Shakin' Stevens had pulled out, so we had to prepare ourselves to be on telly the next day."

Culture Club were right at the forefront of the second "British Invasion" – when, for the first time since the Beatles, UK groups began making a sustained assault on the American charts. It began with Human League's 'Don't You Want Me' reaching US No.1 in early 1982, swiftly followed by Duran Duran, Tears For Fears, Eurythmics, Wham!, Culture Club and Dexy's Midnight Runners, all hitting the US top slot.

✳ ✳ ✳

Dexy's Midnight Runners followed up their first No.1 (1980's *Mean Streets*-era 'Geno') with 'Come on Eileen', and Kevin Rowland was in no doubt about the show's importance, reflecting in 2012: "Going to *Top of the Pops* was always a great thing for me. I watched it since I was a kid – I loved it. I never took it for granted." Fittingly, it was an appearance by Kevin Rowland's Dexy's, during their raggle-taggle gypsy phase, that resulted in one of the best-remembered *Top of the Pops* moments ever.

To follow up 'Eileen', Dexy's recorded Van Morrison's soulful tribute 'Jackie Wilson Said...'. The single reached No.5, and there – right behind Kevin Rowland on the band's *Top of the Pops* appearance was a picture: *not* of the man who had given us 'Reet Petite' and 'Higher & Higher', but rather that of portly darts champion *Jocky* Wilson!

David Jensen was presenting that night: "*That* famous moment, when Dexy's played their 'Jackie Wilson' hit with a backdrop featuring 'Jocky Wilson'...! Well, I pointed out the mistake in rehearsals to the team, but for some reason it went ahead, but as always, the *Pops* is bigger than the sum of its parts – and it's just become part of the show's folklore."

Fondly remembered for OTT videos and elaborate stage-wear, Adam & the Ants became the first bona-fide pop sensations of the new decade, when their 1981 'Stand & Deliver' became the first single of the 1980s to enter the charts at No.1. Adam belonged to a generation that had literally grown up with the programme: "*Top of the Pops* is an artist's ultimate challenge... There's no preferential treatment for anybody – you just go on and perform. It reflects any discotheque at any period of time, it is unpretentious and still the country's classic pop show."

It was in August 1981 that U2 made their debut on the programme promoting 'Fire'. But as Bono laughed later: 'We must be the only band to appear on *Top of the Pops* whose single actually went *down* the following week!" The band's drummer Larry Mullen Jr. admitted he had begun his musical apprenticeship playing a practice pad and watching drummers hard at work on *Top of the Pops* every week.

U2's producer, Steve Lillywhite, went on to marry Kirsty MacColl – who was herself no stranger to the show. But as plugger Maurice Gallagher remembered, appearing on *Top of the Pops* wasn't always as exotic as it looked on the television: "When Kirsty was appearing on *TOTP* performing 'There's a Boy Works Down the Chip Shop (Swears He's Elvis)', her guitarist came up to me after the first rehearsal and asked if I could fix it so that there were no close ups of him. Now this is the opposite to what you usually get. You expect a whinge from the guitarist that there's no shot of him when he does his solo. So I had to ask the guitarist why and he said, 'I'm claiming the dole and I don't want them to see me!'"

This was the era of Wham!, Culture Club, Eurythmics, Soft Cell and the gold-suited ABC – whose Martin Fry spoke fondly of his *TOTP* debut to Stuart Maconie: "A real nervous experience, a real euphoric experience. Just the feeling that you've been watching *Top of the Pops* since you were two years-old. So to contribute, to be on it, was mind-boggling."

Mike Score from A Flock of Seagulls had a more particular memory of appearing on the programme: "We were doing 'Wishing' (No.10, 1982) and I was *really* nervous. And one of the girl dancers said 'Why don't you smile more?' I told her I was nervous, and she kindly said 'Just look at me when you're on – I'll make you smile!'

"So there we were, playing live, and I looked at her dancing behind the camera, and she lifted up her top! Now that *did* make me smile! But when I got home my girlfriend wanted to know what had made me smile so much when I'd spent all day telling her how nervous I was about appearing – she never did find out."

Tragically, though *TOTP* continued to showcase many fine artists, this was also the era of the Fixx, Goombay Dance Band, Marilyn, Jimmy the Hoover, Toto Coeleo, Classix Nouveaux, Belouis Some and, of course, Seona Dancing – although Ricky Gervais's smooth, synth-pop duo never actually made it onto the *Pops*, as their 1983 single 'Bitter Heart' only reached No.70.

Soft Cell's Marc Almond *did* make it though: "My life changed when we went on *Top of the Pops*. I still lived in a bedsit in Leeds. The next day everyone's attitude changed. Love me, kill me, fuck me, marry me!"

In June 1981, as riots threatened to rip the UK apart, came the most prescient single of the year: the Specials' 'Ghost Town', whose eerie, claustrophobic video captured the mood of a nation. As it happened though, the group's *TOTP* appearance happened to coincide with the programme's 900th edition – and for this flagship edition the BBC had decided to bring back one of the show's original hosts, David Jacobs – who after Terry Hall's dour rendition of Jerry Dammers' bleak anthem commented: "Oh dear, that wasn't very cheery was it?"

✳ ✳ ✳

If controversy had another name, it would probably be Malcolm McLaren. After fuelling the incendiary Sex Pistols in the 1970s, the Svengali of Pop courted further outrage by employing teenager Annabella Lwin as singer with his latest pop outrage, Bow Wow Wow. The furore was due as much to McLaren's decision to release the group's cassette recordings and promote home taping, as it was to having Annabella pose nude on their LP cover.

But all was not well within the group's ranks either, as Annabella recalled at an early *Top of the Pops* appearance: "I was going to the loo, when I bumped into an actress whose mum owned a theatre school. We were surprised at seeing each other and asked 'What are you doing here?' She told me she was one of the dancers in the audience for *TOTP* that night. Rather smugly, I told her I was doing a song on stage with a band, she quickly said 'I auditioned for that band you're singing in, but then didn't everybody!' It was around the same time that the guys in the band had already told me they weren't sure about me as lead singer, saying: 'You don't seem committed enough...' I mean, I was fourteen years old!"

Depeche Mode made their *Top of the Pops* debut in 1981 – but it has to be said that the Basildon quartet did not make for the most arresting television. Singer Dave Gahan did move, but the remaining three just stood there, planted behind their plinkity-plonk keyboards. They were on to promote their first hit, 'Just Can't Get Enough' – which I, not very presciently, reviewed for *Melody Maker*. My entire review ran thus: "I can. You will." Depeche Mode went on to have, at the last count, 43 hit singles...

Of all the plinkity–plonk acts of the 80s, Yazoo – the group Vince Clarke formed on quitting Depeche Mode in 1982 – were among the most engaging. This was due in no small part to the gutsy singing of Alison Moyet. Yazoo's first hit was the beguiling 'Only You'; but the duo stayed together for barely a year, before Vince went off to Erasure and "Alf" to a glittering solo career. But Alison always remained riven by self-doubt, as was clear when she spoke to Dave Roberts in 2013: "I remember doing *TOTP*, which was effectively my first TV. The clapping at the start was so loud I couldn't hear my playback, so when my first line comes on, I'm still at the back of the stage. And then, when I do get going, I realise I haven't worked out what I'm going to do with my feet. So I shuffle a bit, and then I didn't know what to do with my hands. I was literally making it up as I went along."

Luckily, no such anxieties troubled the all-male machismo of the guitar-led bands. From the ashes of Deep Purple arose... Gillan, and the Heavy Metal monsters, fronted by the Purps' singer Ian, did surprisingly well on the singles charts of the early 1980s. Bassist John McCoy recalled: "I did *TOTP* numerous times with Gillan, so we *must* have been successful! One notable appearance was when we got a call to appear in the middle of a looooooong tour and of course you say 'Yes, not a problem, we'll fly back on our only day off and hang around Television Centre all day'...! That was all except our guitarist Bernie Torme who refused to go. I think in fact he was using the occasion to try and get some cash out of Ian and his manager... We begged and pleaded, but Bernie stuck to his guns... so we go to do the show, where I attempted to mime *both* guitar parts *and* bass parts! Very Silly! I think the song was 'Mutually Assured Destruction' – catchy title, but then that was the phrase the USA and Russia were using at the time."

Metal legends Iron Maiden made their *TOTP* debut in 1980, as manager Rod Smallwood recalled: "We had previously told our label EMI that we would *never* do *Top of the Pops* unless we did it live! After all, we were a *metal* band not a pop outfit. 'Running Free' came out in February 1980 and we were asked on... Well nobody since the Who had done it live since 1974, but we stuck in and said 'No Live... No Maiden!' In the end they agreed!

"In 1996, 'Falling Down' hit the chart and we were asked on the show again. As we were touring at the time we suggested we film it on location... in Israel! We did it on top of the ancient Masada plateau, where the Hebrews held out against the Romans, eventually sacrificing themselves. We had to cable-car tons of equipment up the sheer walls of Masada and play on top of the ancient bath-house with helicopters swooping in around us. *TOTP* insisted on their logo being in shot, so we had to stick these logos onto 2000 year-old walls. We went over budget on this to EMI's dismay, it cost £40,000 – but it was worth it to get on the show on Iron Maiden's terms!"

In November 1982 *Top of the Pops* had to face its biggest rival since *Ready! Steady! Go!* in the 1960s, when the newly-launched Channel 4 aired their teatime pop show, *The Tube*. In the event it's no wonder that *Tube* producer Malcolm Gerrie was scathing when asked about the competition by Phil Sutcliffe in 1991: "The *Pops* is glitzy, professional, lamely directed, and has the worst presenters on television… It used to be essential viewing, but now the polemic of pop has changed. Kids want to go out and dance and … they're interested in icons, events: Madonna live on Sky; Sinead saying rude words at the MTV awards. They don't talk about 'the Top Twenty'. The chart isn't news any more. What *Top of the Pops* is really up against is the Who Gives a Fuck? factor."

But sheer weight of numbers ensured that the BBC programme could afford to maintain the popular high-ground. Michael Hurll had taken over from Robin Nash as producer in 1980, and talking five years later, Hurll was still clearly unconcerned: "There is no opposition to talk of. The show's status and popularity with its audience is almost by default… People talk about *The Tube*, but it only gets 0.7 million viewers, whereas [we get] 8-10 million regularly – to me there's just no contest."

There was, indeed, something about *Top of the Pops*, and its pedigree, that made it almost unassailable. Plugger Allan James remembered: "From day one in my role of promotion, I would say *every* artist, from UK acts making their TV debut, to established international artists, would always plead: 'Get us on *TOTP*!' This would include all USA clients. Not only pop stars, but critics' favourites like Steely Dan, and *major* rock acts including Bryan Adams, Foreigner, Van Halen, the Cars etc. It was always: 'Get us on, and we'll be there.' They *all* knew, and understood, the importance and power of *TOTP*. For example, Elton always flew into London from Europe whenever he was booked, never ever questioning the travel, time or expense. It was the same for all UK artists – Justin Hayward, Yes, Rainbow, Whitesnake, Eurythmics, Slade etc. They all knew that the right performance on *TOTP* guaranteed a bigger hit single, which increased their profile, and that helped album sales. Plus, especially throughout the 70s and 80s, they all appreciated the hospitality of the BBC Club…"

The Hollies' *Pops* appearances spanned three decades, including that historic first show – and their drummer, Bobby Elliott, agreed enthusiastically about those "fringe benefits": "Eventually, doing *TOTP* became a sideshow. The show was a device to get to where the real action was – the BBC Club! I loved drinking and socialising there before and after the show. A big long bar dotted with actors, newsreaders, musicians; people from other BBC shows mixed and caroused in a relaxed friendly atmosphere. Later, in 1988, when 'He Ain't Heavy…' topped the charts again, and we performed on the show a few more times, I returned to the club, but it was not the same. It all seem a bit threadbare, faceless and uncared for. Times had changed. I just drank my pint and went home…

"We had so many hits in the 1960s – more than any other band, including the Beatles – that we seemed to be on most weeks. If we were working overseas the Beeb would make a film or video of our performance to slot into the weekly schedule. Sadly some BBC type decided to wipe all the video tapes from the early Manchester shows through to about 1968. He thought that the tape could be put to better use than all that pop dross, like gardening programmes etc. He actually believed that he was doing the Corporation a favour!"

Despite all the fluctuating fashions and bewildering byways that pop music had explored since *Top of the Pops* began, perhaps its continuing appeal – like that of its near-contemporary *Private Eye* magazine – lay in its resolutely unchanging format. The show *always* ended with that week's No.1 record. And that record could *only ever* get to the top of the chart by selling more copies than any other during that week.

There may have been detours and hiccups, but primarily *Top of the Pops* concentrated on records which were on the rise. Mind you, this was back in the day when singles were purchased in record stores, and their progress was dictated by weekly incremental sales. So a hit single would enter the charts and then slowly and steadily rise or fall, unlike today when initial sales may result in a high entry only for it to drop out of sight equally quickly.

Installed as producer at the beginning of the new decade, Michael Hurll is remembered as "a bit of taskmaster". But then Hurll's brief was a fairly challenging one: to breathe life into a format which had become – understandably after 16 years in a notoriously fickle industry – just a tad lifeless.

It was Hurll who successfully re-negotiated the deal with the Musicians' Union, which saw the end of the expensive *TOTP* Orchestra. It was not before time, but at long last bands were now allowed to record their own version, of their own song, for the programme.

In addition to the orchestra, another sign of the new regime was the introduction of a new dance troupe. *TOTP* stalwart Flick Colby was happy to see the back of Legs & Co. and thought that Zoo, the new mixed dance troupe of 20, would fit happily into the new format. Making their debut at the end of 1981, Zoo proved a far more flexible outfit – but choreographing the group's routines brought Colby into direct conflict with producer Hurll, and soon Zoo were no more, and the *Top of the Pops* cameras were busy barging into the audience to find suitably photogenic and fun-loving faces.

The studio audience had always been very much a part of the whole *Top of the Pops* experience. And the show remained *the* key place for fans to see their idols in the flesh, and to be seen themselves when the show was broadcast. So the decision to position professional dancers among the studio crowd, even putting them on rostrums, thereby placing them above the dancing public, was poorly received at the time. The *stars* were surely the only ones who should be above the punters, and as the decade progressed, those stars were becoming glossier and ever more exotic.

One band who seemed tailor-made for the 80s, and for the videos that characterised their fashionable music, was Duran Duran. The band's playboy image was enhanced by the exotic locations chosen for their early 80s hits 'Hungry Like a Wolf', 'Save A Prayer'. But it was 1982's 'Rio', with Duran swanning round the Caribbean on a yacht, that was dubbed "the video that kickstarted the 80s". Video producer Scott Millaney remembered: "They were good looking guys and very ambitious. They always saw themselves as a visual band... the videos did all the touring for them. They were probably the first band for ages to break around the world without going on the road."

As the 80s speeded along on a puff of white powder and a spritz of champagne, it seemed that pop style was more exotic than at any time since the glam 70s. And right at the head of the Yuppie pack was Duran Duran, whose John Taylor later admitted: "I never wanted to be a musician; I just wanted to be a pop star! I just wanted to go on *Top of the Pops*, really, and if being a pop star meant you had to go up and down the M1 in the back of a transit van for 10 years, I didn't want to know."

Duran's Simon Le Bon admitted to Jeff Simpson that *TOTP* had even played a significant role in his relationship with his father. They hadn't spoken to each other since Simon announced that he was joining a band: "And it was only when that first *Top of the Pops* was shown that my dad called up and I spoke to him for the first time since joining Duran Duran. He said: 'Well, I guess you're doing all right then Simon, aren't you?'"

Half a decade on from 'Bohemian Rhapsody', and with Thatcherism in the ascendant, it was clear that the way an act looked had as much impact as how they sounded – particularly when it came to the all-powerful *Top of the Pops*. Probably the most influential video makers of that era were ex-10cc members Godley & Creme, who fashioned memorable mini-movies for such acts as Duran Duran, the Police and Frankie Goes To Hollywood. Though perhaps their most striking video of all was the astonishing 'Cry', made to accompany their own modest 1985 hit, which consisted simply of a series of black and white faces, shedding a tear as they morphed into one another.

Hard to believe now, but at the time of its American launch in August 1981, MTV had a library of just 100 videos to draw upon! But soon, Michael Jackson's 1983 'Thriller' video would be seen everywhere, helping to hurl his all-conquering album into the stratosphere. In recent years, the sheer scale of Jackson's success has been downplayed; but no other album had ever generated hits on that scale; and – like it or not – no other album will *ever* replicate the success of *Thriller*.

To this day, no one is entirely clear how many copies *Thriller* has sold (estimates range between 50 and 80 million). But what is certain, is that much of its success was due to the promo videos that accompanied each of the album's record-breaking eight hit singles.

MTV Europe arrived in 1987 – with Dire Straits kicking things off with 'Money For Nothing' – which, along with Peter Gabriel's 'Sledgehammer', introduced the spellbinding blend of stop-motion and animation. But it was Robert Palmer's 1986 video for 'Addicted To Love', wherein the dashing singer sings in front of a black-clad female band, which has since been called "the most copied video ever".

When push came to shove, even *Top of the Pops* was forced to yield to the power of the promo. Of course, the appeal of video for an act – particularly an American act – was that they could now "go global" without even leaving their home city. The first screening of a promo video by a major act now became an event – although the novelty rapidly wore off.

Pops' veteran Johnnie Stewart expressed his doubts in the mid-80s: "You do have to be awfully careful in the way you use these new toys; there comes a time when it can start to get slightly out of hand... A band physically performing is much better than all the video trickery there'll ever be."

One act who enjoyed a particularly thrilling *TOTP* night was Junior: "It was back in '82, and 'Mama Used To Say' had just charted and there I was on *Top of the Pops*! I could hardly believe it. It got even more insane when there was a knock on my dressing room door, and there stood... Paul McCartney! He then handed me a copy of the single and asked me to sign it for him! It transpired that he had been driving down Oxford Street and heard it on Radio 1. He went crazy for it, and called my record label, and they told him I was doing the *Pops* that very day. So he literally drove down to the studios to find me. I was blown away – it just didn't get any better than that!"

With five UK No.1s between 1979 and 1983, the Police were one of the biggest British bands of the era – even going so far as to follow in the Beatles' footsteps and play Shea Stadium. The blonde trio seemed to be everywhere in early 80s. But newsreel footage of the troubles in Northern Ireland incorporated in the video for their 1981 hit, 'Invisible Sun', was deemed "too political" for the *Pops*.

Elvis Costello fashioned his 1983 album *Punch the Clock* for commercial success, recruiting producers Langer & Winstanley (Madness, Dexy's, Teardrop Explodes), but it was the shopping for *Pops* that stuck in Clive Langer's memory: "before he went on *Top of the Pops* he had to go out to buy a Gucci jumper!"

When *Goodbye Cruel World* arrived the following year ("Congratulations, you've just purchased our worst album!" Elvis wrote on the album's 2004 re-release) Daryl Hall was recruited for the album's first single, 'The Only Flame in Town'. Reminiscing, Elvis later wrote: "Daryl made the rest of us look as if we had just crawled out of a hedge. My humour wasn't helped by the record company representative shrieking at the make-up girl: 'Make him look handsome!' as I was about to go under the pancake. Ah! The Eighties."

The act that most benefitted from Langer's presence as producer were the north London fun-boys, Madness. The nutty boys dominated those early 80s single charts with 15 Top Five singles – though 'House of Fun' was their only

No.1. Young and exuberant, they relished taking the mickey out of the rather stiff atmosphere Michael Hurll had brought to the programme. Suggs remembered some run-ins with Hurll, but also recalls the producer allowing them to bring a car into the studio to promote 'Driving In My Car'.

New technology meant that, from the early 1980s onwards, you no longer had to be glued to the television every Thursday evening to get your weekly pop fix. Home video recorders and the decreasing cost of tapes (that would be VHS rather than Betamax then...) meant that you could tape the show, watch your favourites over and over, and keep the video as a permanent souvenir.

Thanks to home video, we can now marvel again at the majority of those 1980s programmes. The BFI's Dick Fiddy: "It wasn't that someone woke up to the value of these things. As with most things, it was financial. The technology actually helped the decision to keep this stuff, so there's very little that's disappeared from the end of the 70s. By the mid-80s there was an awareness: people want to buy stuff on VHS; there were the early stirrings of repeat channels; and, for example, when Channel 4 launched in 1982 one if its first major documentary series was on the 60s. Part of Channel 4's policy was to have a coherent policy on archive television."

While it was a decade marked by technical innovation, the 1980s did not mean the end of the novelty single. With a little help from Noel Edmonds on Radio 1, actor Keith Michell found himself as the voice of Captain Beakey. The Goombay Dance Band's 'Seven Tears' sounded like a sea shanty from a bunch of Thuggee bandits. While folkie Fred Wedlock enjoyed an unlikely hit as 'The Oldest Swinger in Town'.

And, lest we forget, it was in 1981 that Joe Dolce's 'Shaddap You Face' kept Ultravox and their haunting 'Vienna', off the No.1 slot. Other distinguished No.2s included 'Brown Sugar" (kept off the top by Dawn's 'Knock Three Times'); Oasis and 'Wonderwall' (Robson & Jerome's 'I Believe'); perhaps saddest of all, Bowie's 'Jean Genie' *and* John & Yoko's 'Happy Xmas (War Is Over)' both of which were destined to lag behind Little Jimmy Osmond's 'Long Haired Lover From Liverpool'.

One of the more memorable *TOTP* moments of the decade also occurred in 1981, when in January, Phil Collins appeared to promote his debut solo hit 'In the Air Tonight'. It was the start of an incredible run of solo successes, which saw the (and I'm sure he'd be the first to acknowledge the description) short, balding, Genesis drummer dominate the UK and US charts throughout the 1980s. But, aside from the poignant performance, what made Phil's solo *TOTP* debut so memorable was a tin of paint... Sitting somewhat incongruously on his piano, it was taken as a reference to the break-up of Phil's first marriage, when his wife had allegedly left him for a painter and decorator.

* * *

Hard to believe it now, but this was still a period when the music press exerted an enormous amount of power – not just *Smash Hits*, but the weeklies *Melody Maker, NME, Record Mirror* and *Sounds*. And they needed new acts to write about every week, which perhaps helped account for *Top of the Pops* appearances by Blue Rondo A La Turk, Kissing the Pink, JoBoxers, Haysi Fantayze, King Kurt, Roman Holiday... And, of course, Bardo, the UK's entry for the 1982 Eurovision Song Contest – who, despite being energetically promoted by the *Pops*, came 7th, with 'One Step Further'.

One notable contribution from the music press was poacher-turned-gamekeeper Chrissie Hynde, an ex-*NME* contributor who was transformed into the smouldering leader of the Pretenders. One of the band's 1980 performances is particularly poignant, when you look at the original four-piece line-up and realise that, within months, two of the band would be dead.

The launch of the Compact Disc in 1982 marked another technical advance by the record industry – giving grateful fans the opportunity to re-buy all the music they'd owned for years. In 1983, there were only 11 licensed CD pressing plants; but then eastern Europe kicked in, and CD piracy became the issue that dominated the industry – in much the same way as home taping had, and downloading eventually would.

Legendary for ground-breaking albums like *Tubular Bells*, Mike Oldfield also enjoyed a couple of hit singles, guaranteeing him *TOTP* appearances. The best-known was 1983's 'Moonlight Shadow', with vocals from Maggie Reilly, who laughed: "We had flown in late at night to an empty Heathrow – yes, there really was a time you could do that. We had been touring Europe where it was really, really sunny. We spent the night at a hotel somewhere in Hammersmith. I went down for breakfast next morning to find all the guys laughing at me. Overnight, I had come out in some kind of heat rash all over my face and it was swelling up. Needless to say, the guys went to the run-through and I spent the day in hospital trying to stop the swelling. In the end, the very able make-up department at the BBC came to my rescue and managed to camouflage my face enough to get through – oh and I did wear a hat, so that helped.

"But it was really hard to keep my eyes open and stop scratching at the rash – thank God there was no HD television back then! I was taken to the bar afterwards and medicated. All the dancers were there being chatted up by the band – and six months later in my kitchen, I was looking out of the window and the girl next door was doing the same. After a couple of days we realized we'd met before! She was one of the *TOTP* dancers, Sandy Bourne, who went on to *Starlight Express*... I still get cards at Christmas; small world eh?"

By the time *Top of the Pops* celebrated its 1000th edition, on 5 May 1983, it had come a mighty long way from that disused church in Manchester. A plethora of presenters were on hand to introduce – live in the studio – Spandau Ballet, Thompson Twins, Human League, the Beat, Heaven 17, Blancmange and Funboy Three – well, it *was* the 80s...

Spandau drummer John Keeble recalled his surprise when the band first appeared on the show in 1980: "I was just astounded how small the studio was, I'd always looked at it on the television and thought it was some huge auditorium. It then struck me just how clever the people behind the programme were, as they made it come to life on the screen and have it a sense of electricity."

With late 70s punk now established as Year Zero in rock history, the beginning of the 1980s saw pop increasingly looking over its shoulder. On the back of Paul Weller's avowed enthusiasm, and the film of *Quadrophenia*, came the Mod Revival with young guns like the Lambrettas and Secret Affair landing *Top of the Pops* appearances. Ageing Mods watched with sagging jaws (and bellies) as the pop monster began devouring its own tail. Andy Peebles told Shaun Tilley: "I'm of the original Mod generation but I bow the knee particularly to the 2-Tone stuff, a lot of the other bands, I thought were playing at it, just because you're wearing a parka with a fur collar doesn't make you a Mod!"

Allied to the new Mods came neo-psychedelia, as colourful 80s hippies like Nick Nicely, Mood Six and the Dukes Of Stratosphear emerged. In a similar, though longer-lasting, patchouli-scented vein came Teardrop Explodes, Echo & the Bunnymen and Siouxsie & the Banshees – all citing the music of 15 years before as an influence.

But of all the new psychedelic bands, one of the most successful was Marillion

– and such was their debt to that which had gone before, that they took their name from *The Silmarillion*, Tolkien's "follow-up" to *The Lord of the Rings*. Singer Fish recalled: "It was the late summer of 1985 and 'Lavender' was riding high in the charts. We were mid-tour, and my voice just went – completely *gone*! We had to blow gigs out, which we *never* did, but then, when we were asked onto the show we were in a bit of a quandary to say the least…

"We had always *hated* the idea of miming on the TV – after all we were a *rock* band on a pop show, so we had to show a bit of grit! We came up with the idea of doing a 'Bob Dylan' and showing the lyric sheets to camera, like Bob had done in *Don't Look Back*. It was tongue in cheek, but it meant I could mouth the words as best I could. Well, it worked, and it was smiles all round, and in a way it was a finger up to the mimers. But, no matter what, never *ever* miss a *Top of the Pops*!"

In the 1970s, the end of civilisation as we knew it had been the Sex Pistols. For the new decade, it was Frankie Goes To Hollywood. Their 1984 No.1 'Relax' remains infamous for being excluded from the Radio 1 airwaves by Mike Read, who took offence at the Scallies' homo-erotic lyrics.

It was a record that demonstrated both the power of controversy and the power of the producer. The radio ban naturally increased record sales – but because it was a blanket BBC ban, it meant that despite 'Relax' remaining at the top for five weeks, the Frankies themselves remained unseen on *TOTP*. The video (all leather bondage and suggestive imagery) also went unscreened, but eventually the Beeb relented, and Frankie Goes To Hollywood were seen performing their controversial hit on the year-end Christmas roundup.

Despite the sexual controversy they had unleashed, Holly Johnson told Jeff Simpson that the group's real worry was rather more prosaic: "The record company were really stingy and we had to go to them and say: 'Look, if we do *Top of the Pops* we can't sign on any more, you have to put us on a wage.' So that was the most serious implication for me of being on *Top of the Pops*."

The record producer's power was evident from Trevor Horn's fashioning of the tectonic-sounding hit. Having seen Frankie Goes To Hollywood perform an early version of the song on *The Tube*, he decided to re-record 'Relax' with stellar musicians from Ian Dury's Blockheads rather than the Liverpudlians. In fact, the only group member who could be heard on that breakthrough single was singer Holly Johnson. Frankie Goes To Hollywood went on to enjoy two further No.1s in 1984 alone: the equally controversial 'Two Tribes', and the "ah, they're not so threatening after all" ballad 'Power Of Love'.

Holly Johnson felt that there were definitely two sides to the *Top of the Pops* experience. "There's what you see on the screen – the glamour, the glitz, the fantastic pop stars, and then in the 80s there was the dreary BBC Television Centre and the extras from *Tenko* that you had to share dressing room space with. And the windowless dressing rooms that were really miserable and corporate, a bit like going back to school!"

✳ ✳ ✳

Denied the No.1 slot by 'Two Tribes', was actor Nigel Planer – performing as Neil from BBC2's "alternative comedy" *The Young Ones*: "My experience with *TOTP* was a steep and wonderful learning curve. It was great to be a pop star, but only in character. So I could see what the crazy world of pop was like, but not have to take the consequences.

"Well it was in 1984 when 'Hole in My Shoe' was No.2 in the charts – neil would moan 'even my hit single is a number two', when talking about his poo! I was booked to go on *Top of the Pops* and I needed to rehearse with the camera and sound because – horror of horrors – I was going to sing and speak live! It was impossible to mime to all the spoken bits effectively, and also I wanted to stick in some extra lines like 'listen to the lyrics Paul Weller'!

"At the time I was in the middle of filming the series *Roll Over Beethoven* in Nottinghamshire... Many phone calls between agents, producers, pluggers, record execs, pluggers, directors and pluggers happened, to try and ensure that I would make the camera rehearsal for *TOTP* at 6pm. A helicopter was booked to take me down to Battersea Heliport station. It was an exciting day and a first for me – from none to two helicopter rides on the same day. I was assured the journey to London was only 45 minutes or so and so we confirmed *TOTP*.

"The helicopter zipped me down to London, it was a fantastic ride – we snaked along the length of the Thames. There is glass below your feet, so I could see the landmarks zooming between my legs – it was almost erotic. Then we landed at Battersea. Not bad time, we had about half an hour, forty minutes to spare – Battersea to Shepherd's Bush, should be possible. Nip through a few back streets... I rushed out of the helicopter, bending over too much under the rotating blades as every one does, imagining I was Nick Nolte or De Niro in some tough movie. I checked out and into the Battersea heliport car park .

"A stretch limo had been booked to pick me up from the heliport. A long stretch limo. A *very* long stretch limo with just me in it. So long that it could not negotiate more than a gentle 70-odd degree turn. It was coming up to six o'clock and we were hitting the worst of west London's rush hour.... This was in the days before mobiles, remember, so there was no way to ring ahead and say – I'm on my way. Poor lonely pop star, sitting in his limo all alone, with schoolgirls pointing through the window at him, laughing as they walked home, faster than the traffic.

"Panic at the other end when eventually I arrived with minutes to spare. Directors, pluggers, producers, agents, execs, pluggers... I managed to disobey pop star protocol and walked onto the set to talk directly to cameramen and sound, who obligingly scribbled notes into their camera scripts. They understood pretty quickly that I didn't want the usual *TOTP* pan from behind artist to in front of artist from left to right...They were fine. No problem, as ever, between the people who make stuff. Problem was the whole pecking order, and style of the mammoth business interests behind the scenes. Definitely nicer being a pretend person than a real one. It was worth putting up with the wig for that."

✱ ✱ ✱

Despite such heroic efforts to appear live, video remained a key ingredient of *Top of the Pops*. 'Bohemian Rhapsody' may be the Queen video everyone remembers, but as they continued their global triumph throughout the 1980s, the band produced some equally memorable videos for TV. One of the best was the *Coronation Street* spoof that accompanied 1984's 'I Want To Break Free', which had the quartet all dragged up; though one wonders how many hours it took to teach Freddie Mercury to operate such a prosaic item as a hoover!

Dave Stewart and Annie Lennox, who had helped fuel the second British Invasion as Eurythmics, made six memorable *Top of the Pops* appearances during the 1980s, but equally impressive were those Eurythmics videos, with Annie happily gender-bending.

Singled out by Elvis Costello as *the* songwriter to watch, Aztec Camera's Roddy Frame went from being the darling of the indie world, to a major label, and then onto his favourite television show: "Appearing on the show is something I always looked forward to, from the day I was watching *Top of the Pops* and saw Roy Wood and Wizzard do 'Ball Park Incident' back in 1972. Appearing on it was the fulfillment of an ambition, I just promised myself I'd be there."

The programme's appeal allowed it to span the generations, and every facet of the musical spectrum. Leee John of Imagination had equally fond memories as a viewer and performer, and happily recalled the transition: "As a kid back in the 70s I would watch the show with the family – and, as mum did the ironing, I would just dream the dream of one day *appearing* on the show. It was great escapism, all those unreachable stars: the Sweet, Wizzard, the Jackson 5, Sweet Sensation – it was just wonderful to watch. I just remember thinking 'I want to be like that one day'.

"By the end of the decade, I'd got a job as a messenger boy at the BBC – and was one step nearer my dream. It all got a bit too much though when I heard that Stevie Wonder was on the show, and I sneaked in to take a look. I was slung out! A few years later 'Body Talk' hit the charts at No. 44 and we got the call – and there I was! This time I got to stay for the whole show and my dream had come true. I didn't realise what an impact that one appearance would have, but I was walking down Tottenham Court Road in London a few days later, and behind me were a trail of newly-born Imagination fans – even a few buses stopped, it was incredible!

"As time went on we got to be known for our OTT outfits, but of course there was a pressure to get more outrageous with every performance. We outdid ourselves with the infamous jockstraps incident. We didn't wear them in rehearsals, just strode out clad in them for the show itself – and before anyone could say anything, we were live. They enhanced the 'fruits of loom' somewhat and caused a bit of a fuss into the bargain!"

By the mid-80s, *Top of the Pops* had acquired some new faces: Radio 1's Steve Wright, Peter Powell, Janice Long, Bruno Brookes and Mark Page had joined their illustrious predecessors. Steve Wright admitted: "I watched the show for eight years, every week, with my mum and dad. Eyes and mouth open wide! My favourite performance, I remember, was Mud doing 'Lonely This Christmas' with Les Gray holding a dummy Santa and very, *very* false snow falling on the band. Little did I know that one day I would present the show. I say this and mean it: what a *privilege*."

On her way to overtaking the redoubtable Nana Mouskouri as the world's best-selling female vocalist, Madonna made her *Top of the Pops* debut in 1984.

Steve Wright laughed as he recalled: "Madonna was rehearsing 'Like A Virgin' in the studio, and I was having a bit of a day of it. To make things worse my mum had been going on to me that she was making a special dinner for me and not to be late... So, I found myself saying to the Queen of Pop 'Excuse me, do you think you could hurry it up a bit? My mum is making stew for dinner!'"

Coming back later in the year, Madonna appeared in a vivid pink wig, a fact that didn't help Michael Hurll's brand recognition: "I thought she was somebody totally different," he confessed to Jeff Simpson. "I actually ignored her and thought it was some mad woman coming round the studio!" Which might go some way to explaining why it would be a further 11 years before the Queen of Pop returned to the *Pops* studio.

Bruno Brookes, who hosted his first show on 13 September 1984, told Shaun Tilley: "My mum used to tape the show when I was a kid... an iconic programme! And I was absolutely *petrified* presenting that first show, I literally broke out in a cold sweat. At the end, I went out and got *completely* hammered!" Bruno's *Pops* debut had a pretty representative mid-80s line-up: Orchestral Manoeuvres in the Dark, Ray Parker Jr., Level 42, U2, Shakin' Stevens, Depeche Mode, Miami Sound Machine, and on video, at No.1: Stevie Wonder, just getting into his six-week run at the top with 'I Just Called to Say I Love You'.

It was while he was at home watching television on 24 October 1984 that Bob Geldof first became moved – and then angered – by the harrowing scenes of the famine in Ethiopia. Calling in favours from the entire music industry, Geldof hurriedly put together Band Aid. In doing so, he gave that selfish, fashion-obsessed decade a conscience, and the charts their best-selling single to date, with 'Do They Know It's Christmas?' The accompanying video became a regular feature on *TOTP* during its six-week run at the top.

For the show's 1984 Christmas special, something special was required, as Geldof's Band Aid collaborator Midge Ure recalled: "Well, the video had obviously been seen on the show, but they wanted something a bit different for Christmas. So over the three Christmas shows they just filmed the various stars singing along to the record and glued them together at the end – and 'Hey Presto', Band Aid!" Altogether, the Band Aid organisers had hoped to raise £100,000 in the run up to Christmas 1984; as it turned out, the song alone soon raised £10million – and it went on to become a staple of the festive playlist.

Successive generations have created their own Band Aid: the 1989 version featured Bros, Jason Donovan, Wet Wet Wet and Lisa Stansfield among others. In 2004, it was the turn of Keane, Dido, Robbie Williams, Will Young, Katie Melua – and many, many more – to do their bit. Every version so far has reached No.1, and together they have helped raise in excess of £100 million for the Band Aid Trust.

* * *

The dynamic duo of George Michael and Andrew Ridgeley stand proud as the only British act of the 1980s to have three singles reach No.1 in both the UK and USA. Wham! were perfect for *Top of the Pops*; and their bright and breezy pop echoed around discos across the nation. But it was a fluke that landed them their first *TOTP*. Their second single, 'Young Guns', which was inching up the chart, stalled at No. 42 (George Michael: "I was really in the dumps.") But a producer had seen them on *Saturday Superstore*, and even though they were outside the Top 40, he invited Wham! on the show – which helped them ship 30,000 copies the next day.

"*Top of the Pops* has straddled the British music business like a grinning colossus," wrote George Michael's official biographer, Tony Parsons. "More important to the domestic singles market than all the other media outlets put together. *Top of the Pops* is the gateway to the singles charts, the magic lantern that can make all pop dreams come true…" And talking about that fortuitous appearance, George himself admitted "that was the big turning point."

George Michael was already enjoying a solo career while still with Wham!, and in 1985 he featured on no fewer than four records in the Top Twenty: the duo's 'I'm Your Man' and 'Last Christmas'; the Band Aid single; and also as a guest on Elton John's 'Nikita'. The Bushey-born superstar was left in no doubt about the importance of the programme: "Our first appearance on *Top of the Pops* was the second most exciting thing to happen to me, or third if you include being born! It is though, still my favourite show to perform on."

"I could not believe I was there," DJ Dixie Peach told Shaun Tilley about his *TOTP* presenting debut in 1985. "I just thought: can it get any better than this?" He had arrived via Radio Caroline, Radio 1, and the group Mirage, but Dixie was still unprepared for that first occasion: "Walking into the studio at Shepherd's Bush, looking at the cameras, I suddenly realised I was totally out of my depth! I was half expecting to be allowed to cock-up, but *Top of the Pops* was effectively live – that was it, thanks a lot, and I'd be thinking I could have done that better, but they'd say 'No, that was good enough, we're moving on!'

Billy Bragg landed on the show in 1985 when his *Between the Wars* EP reached No.15, prompting a *TOTP* appearance. Bragg's brand of politically-charged folk protest was at odds with the era of big hair, big shoulder pads and Yuppies. Andrew Collins, Bragg's official biographer, later wrote: "Most bands dream of their first *Top of the Pops* appearance. Even today, with the beleaguered show adrift on Friday evenings when it was always a Thursday night fixture, it is a landmark for artist and record company promotions department alike. It was never Billy's dream, partly because he didn't watch it as a teenager, and when he did as a young man he kept seeing Spandau Ballet on it... Plus, of course, the Clash always refused to appear on it, which impressed Billy at the time." Actually, of all the No.1 hits in the programme's 40-plus years, Billy Bragg in 1988 was one of the unlikeliest; mind you, he was singing a Beatle song ('She's Leaving Home') as a double A-side on the back of Wet Wet Wet – all in aid of charity, of course.

"It was Thatcher's Britain. There was money." Janice Long told Jeff Simpson. "People showed off the fact that they had money. And *Top of the Pops* represented what was going on politically. It was *Dynasty* and *Dallas* wasn't it? It was a greedy time, and a terribly ostentatious time – no point in being subtle."

While on the subject of Big Hair, no mullet was bigger or better-known than that of Radio 1 DJ Pat Sharp. "My first appearance was in 1982, when I was introduced as one of the three new kids on the block, along with Gary (Davies) and Janice (Long). Needless to say, presenting *Top of the Pops* was a lifelong ambition. It *is* difficult to appreciate today just what a... privilege it was.

"I can remember being in a dressing room with *every* single famous Radio 1 DJ I had grown up listening to. This was May 1983 for the 1000th edition of the show and I just kept my head down and listened to the various egos taking the piss out of each other! Yes, we were all in the same dressing room! I almost messed up turning Level 42's name around to reflect their chart position – that being No.24 – but just about got it right when I needed to, for the live show they were on.

"For my first ever show I met the Bananarama girls in the corridor, before introducing them with the Fun Boy 3, and I thought they were *so* hot. And of course, he mentioned modestly, I was one of the very few DJs to appear on the *Pops* as a star in my own right – we did it as Pat & Mick a grand total of five times!"

But in fact Pat had been beaten to it by another star DJ back in 1978, as Terry Wogan recalled: "I was never cutting-edge enough to present *TOTP* (lapels too small, ditto flared trousers) but I did perform my hit 'The Floral Dance', which had surged up the charts unexpectedly – to my surprise, and everybody else's! As the brass band played, a phenomenon never to be heard again on the show, I threw flowers to the audience as I sang. And they threw them back…!"

One of the most enduring acts of the era were Pet Shop Boys and Neil Tennant told Dave Roberts that one of his favourite moments from that period was "when we were doing *TOTP* in 1985, we were No.1 with 'West End Girls'. The track started, the camera panned towards us, and Chris hissed from behind me 'Don't look triumphant!'"

Tennant, a seasoned music industry veteran, (well, he wrote for *Smash Hits)*, helped steer Pet Shop Boys to an astonishingly durable career but, ironically, one of Pet Shop Boys' highlights was their 1987 Christmas No.1, a cover of the Elvis song 'Always On My Mind', and the record which kept the Pogues' 'Fairytale Of New York' off the Christmas No.1 slot. Still, it was great to see Shane and the late Kirsty MacColl performing 'Fairytale' on *TOTP* – with Kirsty dutifully substituting "you ass" for "your arse".

One record which *did* reach No.1 in 1987 was T'Pau's 'China In Your Hand', and the band's Carol Decker had nothing but fond memories of the show: "*Top of the Pops* was a British TV institution. Like thousands of kids down the years, I had been glued to the screen every Thursday night, and literally dreamed of appearing on it. So it really was an honour to be invited on.

"I have fond memories of the many appearances that I made with T'Pau on *Top of the Pops.* The first time was performing 'Heart & Soul' when it got to No. 4 – and this was very special, as when it had been previously released it only got to No. 98! We thought it was all over before it began, so it was incredibly exciting and such a relief to finally arrive at the legendary studios at White City. And to see all the personnel: the bossy floor managers, the massive TV cameras gliding around like Daleks, the lights and the logo… and then to hear that famous theme tune fire up as we got ready to record!

"Being on the show with Paul McCartney was particularly exciting; he and Linda sort of adopted me for the day. They said I reminded them of their little redheaded daughter Stella! I remember Paul going to fetch Linda and I coffee from the canteen. It was *disgusting*, in little polystyrene beakers.

"But I suppose my most notable recollection was our first appearance as the nation's No.1 with 'China In Your Hand'. I can't honestly remember which DJ was hosting, I just remember nearly exploding with pride as he announced us… Axing *Top of the Pops* was a sad day for me. It was huge part of, not just my career, but my youth."

✳ ✳ ✳

Writing around that time, long-standing show-watcher Tony Parsons wrote: "What is right with popular music on TV is *Top of the Pops*… It is nothing less than the people's choice. If the masses don't buy it then it will not be shown; if it doesn't get shown it won't get known. How democratic can you get?"

The late John Peel's relationship with the programme was rather more double-edged. Following his grudging appearances in the 1960s, throughout the 1970s Peel cemented his position as the thinking man's DJ and the true champion of all things interesting heard on Radio 1. A list of Peel "firsts" is, in itself, a trailblazing history of British alternative music.

The young Marc Bolan was an early Peel protégé, although the two fell out as Bolan's star ascended in the 1970s. But Bolan's legacy would last long after his death, as plugger John Reed recalled: "The Blow Monkeys' Doctor Robert was a huge fan of Marc Bolan and decided that for the *TOTP* performance of 'It Doesn't Have To Be This Way' he would wear a feather boa – just like Bolan had done on the show many years before. We advised him against it, as it didn't look right outside of the glam rock era. But he wouldn't listen and that night during the recording, he spent the whole time he was singing spitting out feathers!"

With his music cred now unassailable and a certain mellowing that came with age, Peel was persuaded back onto the *Pops* in February 1982 and became a regular host for the remainder of the decade. Nevertheless, his diary revealed him to be "in a highly nervous condition," and worried about how many takes he would take to get it right. "I was introduced and left to say amusing things – which I was quite clearly incapable of. This rattled me. I messed up Takes 2 and 3, completely forgetting the spontaneous drolleries I'd been working on for months and started sweating unpleasantly."

Things fortunately improved, and in conjunction with David Jensen, Peel made his languorous mark on the programme for many years. Moreover, Peel's withering introductions were delightedly at odds with the forced bonhomie of the other presenters – and many were the high and mighty who suffered put-downs from the DJ formerly known as John Ravenscroft. "The best song I've heard since, oooh, teatime, mind you, I had a late tea!" (Duran Duran); "those Sun City boys..." (Queen); "You know Aretha Franklin can make any old rubbish sound good, and I think she just has." (Aretha Franklin & George Michael).

In 1995, Peel was baffled to be asked once again to present *Top of the Pops* – a programme he hadn't graced in eight years. In fact, it was just a ruse to get the DJ, already well on his way to becoming a National Treasure, onto *This Is Your Life*.

David Jensen recalled: "I worked with John Peel a lot, I'm not sure why we were paired together but we just seemed to work well, and John was always trying to crack me up! But we loved the live element: no safety net, and always a real party atmosphere – it just felt like home!

"I championed a lot of bands in the 80s – and a lot of them would do their very first sessions on my Radio 1 show. People such as Culture Club made their debut on my show, and hey presto, a while later I would be introducing them on *Top of the Pops*. The show was a great way to promote my radio show, and it also worked the other way around. It was a win-win situation.

"It became the norm to meet stars from all over the world, but occasionally someone would blow me away, and when Bob Marley played live in the studio I have to admit being *totally* starstruck. The man was just amazing, what a presence! But it was never, ever boring. I recall Tom Petty & the Heartbreakers going into make up and asking for dark circles under their eyes to make them look more rock & roll!

"Of course, being live can have its downside! I was introducing Hot Chocolate once and turned to a girl next to me and asked: 'So, are you a fan?' 'No,' came the swift reply, 'I don't like them at all...!' So with forced grin I went into my link – but hey that's *live*!"

Another regular presenter during the 1980s was Radio 1 DJ Janice Long: "My first one, I was introduced by Peter Powell, along with Pat Sharp and Gary Davies – the 'new faces' of Radio 1. It was 2nd December 1982 and I had to wear an *awful* Radio 1 jacket, like the sort of thing you'd buy at a motorway service station.

"Looking back, it was quite a thing, being the first woman to introduce acts on *Top of the Pops* – and the first act I introduced was U2, 'New Year's Day' – not a bad start!

"Like so many, I grew up watching *TOTP* and all those pivotal moments: Bowie, Bolan... And all of a sudden, *you* are there, introducing the Smiths! I was there when David Bowie came in, and he just took control, directing the cameras, where he wanted the lights placed! And me – in the dressing room next door to David Bowie!

"I remember seeing Bowie doing 'Starman' and thinking I really want to be a part of this, and seeing Marc Bolan and thinking, this music is for me. You would pre-record on Wednesday, to go out on Thursday, and occasionally live. I would shop on the Tuesday at Hyper Hyper in Kensington, but the outfit always ended up costing more than my fee!

"It was a dream time for me: the Smiths, Echo & Bunnymen, then China Crisis, OMD, Teardrop Explodes, Pete Wylie – all from my hometown of Liverpool. The Jesus & Mary Chain, Primal Scream and U2 were just kicking off, I was always disappointed not be on with the Cult... Then you'd finish the show and convene in the famous BBC bar, having a drink with Madness. I mean all the groups... they *all* wanted to be on the show; it was a way of showing everyone that you had arrived!

"Of course, there was some music you just couldn't abide: I remember Michael Crawford was on with 'Music of the Night' from *Phantom of the Opera*, and I said something like 'well somebody must like it!' And Anne Robinson read out a letter complaining on *Points of View*. Pete Wylie was on doing 'Sinful' and I was on with John Peel, who said: 'Well, if that doesn't get to No.1, I will personally come round to your house and break wind!' And we were inundated with complaints. But afterwards Michael Hurll came up and said 'Go on, do something controversial next week!'

"I did think it was really glamorous, though one producer did ask them to move the audience in front of me because I was pregnant: 'Hide that bump, we don't want to see *that*!' And it *was* a long day. You'd begin mid-afternoon with the chart rundown and be *really* lively, like a kid with too much sugar! I loved going into make up and being pampered, then I'd keep it on and go down to the Embassy Club!

"There was that mad juxtaposition – which after all, was reflecting people's taste. It was something that everyone as a family watched, that and *Tomorrow's World*. In fact, Maggie Philbin (who is my ex-sister in law) and I used to dare each other to wear the same outfit: me on *Top of the Pops* following her on *Tomorrow's World*!"

* * *

One tantalising clip from March 1986 has Kate Bush in the studio performing 'Hounds Of Love'. Today, a reclusive and almost mythical figure, it's jarring to see La Bush in grey suit moving and miming and patently loving every moment of the limelight. And what was it with the dry ice? Did the BBC get points for every use? It seemed as though every act of the 1980s was emerging from a "London particular" – often so thick that you struggled to see the act!

Plugger John Reed recalled an especially fraught *TOTP* encounter in 1986: "We were promoting Modern Talking's 'Brother Louie' and had been warned by BMG in Germany that Thomas Anders, the lead vocalist, was managed by his wife – a wealthy German model called Nora, and that she was *extremely* difficult. After the first run, she was glued to a studio monitor and their assistant came over to speak with me. She said Nora was very unhappy because there weren't enough shots of the necklace round Thomas's neck: a huge gold encrusted 'Nora'. I started to laugh as I thought this was a wind-up! But the girl nearly fainted and begged me not to laugh as she would get into trouble. I said I would have a word with the director Brian Whitehouse, who was very nice… At the first break I had a little word in his ear and naturally he told me what they could do with their necklace! Brian told her in no uncertain words that he was the director, he would decide what shot to take – and if she didn't like it, she could take her husband and his necklace and go back to Germany! She was stunned as no one had dared to speak to her like that before and she withdrew sheepishly to the dressing rooms. The performance went ahead and we never saw them again."

Subtlety was definitely not part of the Scott, Aitken & Waterman approach; but success was. Throughout the 1980s, the production trio with the Midas touch dominated the UK charts, and thus *Top of the Pops*. Along with George Martin and (latterly and for all the wrong reasons) Phil Spector, Scott, Aitken & Waterman became the only record producers that most record buyers could probably name.

Behind the board for Dead Or Alive, Hazel Dean, Kylie Minogue, Jason Donovan, Sinitta, Rick Astley, Sonia… S,A&W managed to inject some quality pop frippery into the charts. They recognised the importance of good songs, good record production and good performances. And, even at the height of their powers, Pete Waterman never took anything as given, as he explained to Jeff Simpson: "We never took *Top of the Pops* for granted. We always knew you had three minutes to give it your greatest shot, and the whole combination of what we did was aimed at that three minutes on a Thursday night."

Rick Astley was another act who had grown up watching *Top of the Pops*: "As a kid, watching the show it looked like there thousands of people dancing around. In my naivety, I had thought the studio was rammed full of stages. So when I did my first one I was totally shell-shocked! I couldn't believe how *small* the set was: maybe 80 to a 100 people, and just two small stages. But it didn't spoilt it – and I recall thinking: 'I'm on *what*? It can't be happening!'

"The show played a *massive* part in my career, and when my turn came around once more to be on the show, I gave it everything I had. For someone like me it was the be all and end all.

"I was a huge Smiths fan – they were *so* cool and sort of anti-pop. So I was totally gobsmacked when I met Morrissey on a show, and he insisted he got a photograph with me. I think he did it with others too – but I will never forget that moment." That same photo was used on the 2013 reissue of Morrissey's 'Last of the Famous International Playboys'.

✳ ✳ ✳

With the plethora of "alternative" comedians during the decade, it was no small wonder that the 1980s reminded *TOTP* viewers that the novelty single was not dead: Alexei Sayle, TV's *The Young Ones* and Harry Enfield all appeared in the charts. Rather more strangely, Madonna's producer William Orbit later admitted he was the writer of Enfield's 'Loadsamoney' and had appeared on *Top of the Pops* dressed as a plumber.

It seems that every decade throws up a pop act or two that seem designed to make watching parents wring their hands in horror, while muttering about the end of civilisation and reaching for a stiff drink. In the 60s it was the Rolling Stones; the 70s spawned the Sex Pistols; and you'd have thought that after Frankie Goes To Hollywood, the 80s had already exhausted its shock potential. But no, waiting in the wings – or rather the clubs... or disused airfields... or just fields... was the phenomenon known as House. Or Dance. Or "I must be getting really old!" Or "Are you sure the record isn't stuck?"

Did it all really begin with Paul Hardcastle's 1985 No.1 – the stuttering '19'?

Certainly that single was probably the first time a mass audience had become aware of sampling – and, aside from the Who's 'My Generation', on-disc stuttering.

Like punk, it seemed to industry outsiders that the Acid House explosion had come from nowhere. But with 1988 designated the Second Summer Of Love, it now spread out from Manchester and the Hacienda, onto the nation's front pages. And, then inevitably, into the charts; before progressing to the *Pops*.

M/A/R/R/S 'Pump Up the Volume' was a 1987 No.1, with samples from James Brown, Eric B & Rakim and the Stock, Aitken & Waterman composition 'Roadblock' – which led to a law suit, the first of many involving sampling. S. Express, Yazz, Coldcut, Black Box… all graced the *Top of the Pops* studio with hypnotic, high-energy hits in the late 1980s.

One man who kept a weather eye on all the changes on the pop landscape was Johnny Beerling, who shared his memories of those times with Steve Blacknell: "As Controller of Radio 1 between 1985 and 1993, I always saw *TOTP* as a very useful promotional tool for our network. Let's face it, as the only BBC Radio network facing competition from an increasingly successful chain of commercial stations, we needed all the help we could get. Regular appearances by Radio 1 DJs ensured exposure to that huge Thursday evening audience. And this was a big plus as it served as a constant reminder to the viewers that there was a regular BBC radio station playing their music.

"It wasn't just the main daytime DJ stars who appeared either. Obvious faces like Tony Blackburn, Dave Lee Travis, Noel Edmonds and Gary Davies were sometimes moved aside to make way for unlikely presenters such as John Peel and Kid Jensen, better known on the radio for their enthusiasm for alternative bands. No matter, the call of the magic box lured them all in front of the cameras, where they enthusiastically endorsed the chart hits of the week.

"Where it was of even more help was in 1987 when, after 20 years of our existence, we acquired a Radio 1 FM stereo Network. We managed to arrange a successful tie-up so that we could simulcast the soundtrack of the TV show in stereo on Radio 1. Listeners no longer had to switch on the TV to hear it, they could tune to their favourite radio station and hear it as it happened. Another valuable promotional tie-in.

"So by and large the relationship was mutually beneficial. We got masses of free publicity, while producer Michael Hurll had the use of a number of very well known presenters. However there was one occasion which was hugely embarrassing, this was the banning of Frankie Goes to Hollywood's hit 'Relax'.

"Radio 1 had played it something like 74 times without any complaints before Mike Read stupidly drew attention to the somewhat dubious nature of the lyric on his Breakfast Show, and announced that he would not be playing it. The press picked up on this and the newspapers had a field day at our expense. The upshot was that Radio 1 reluctantly had to ban it. Under the principle of 'one BBC' this meant that *TOTP* also had to ban it, which was somewhat unfortunate as they had already screened it a few times. The whole BBC was somewhat red-faced and embarrassed and I suspect we all lost face in the eyes of the public. How times change, these days it appears in retrospective programmes and no one thinks anything of it.

"That apart, I have nothing but happy memories of that great pop show which started in a converted church in Manchester and finished in TV Centre at Shepherd's Bush. Now both those buildings have gone, along with all those dancing girls and the miming bands and singers. The show was as ephemeral as the music it featured. Fashions and tastes change and all that's left now are the video tapes of days gone by. Those were the days my friend, we thought they'd never end... but sadly they did."

It has to be remembered that with the technology that was available by then, whole orchestras could be simulated from a single keyboard, so that many of the hit acts on *Top of the Pops* during that era were far from visually arresting. A bloke poking at a Roland keyboard did not make for great television, so Black Box recruited the stunning model Katrin Quinol who mimed Loleatta Holloway's vocal in an effort to make 'Ride On Time' more television friendly.

Even so, getting the group on the show was not without incident, as plugger John Reed explained: "Producer Paul Ciani informed me that Loleatta Holloway's lawyers had been in touch and threatened that if the BBC broadcast the record, they would sue! As we all now know the record contained a huge sample of Loleatta's vocal which we discovered had not been cleared by the Italian producers. Paul announced that they were off the show, but thankfully I managed to persuade him to record the track and said we would have something sorted by the time he came to edit the show the following day. Thankfully the legal guys at BMG managed to resolve the problem and the performance got included in the programme and became a huge hit. But it could have been so *very* different."

One bloke who appeared in 1987 and did know a bit about moving around onstage, was Mick Jagger. Mike Smith introduced the Stone, who was making his first *TOTP* appearance in 17 years. To help promote his solo release 'Let's Work', Mick preened and strutted and *mimed*. The resultant performance prompted a comment on the Rolling Stones website "by a mile, the most embarrassing moment *ever* in the Stones history!"

When one of the great *Top of the Pops* debacles occurred around this time, that was all down to miming too. All About Eve were appearing live on the programme during the summer of 1988, but the group's singer, the photogenic Julianne Regan, was unable to mime as planned to 'Martha's Harbour' as the studio playback had broken down. The poor chanteuse had to sit there in silence as the song played.

After all those years, and all those episodes, miming was still an issue on *TOTP*. And many acts took every opportunity to remind viewers that they *were* miming: Marillion's Fish "doing a Bob Dylan" and holding up lyric cue cards; Nick Lowe losing the lyrical plot and grinning through 'I Love the Sound of Breaking Glass'; Mud's Les Gray "singing" with the help of a ventriloquist's dummy; Oasis' Noel and Liam swapping roles ("We were very happy getting pissed in the bar," Noel told Ian Gittins, "knowing that we only had to mime on the programme"); all of Squeeze swapping instruments; Kurt Cobain manifestly miming; the Orb playing chess!…

Martin Page of Tight Fit offered an insight into the draconian Musician Union rules which dictated every appearance of the time, and mentioned a name that still sends shivers down musicians' spines: "Every time Tight Fit were scheduled for *TOTP*, Jive Records asked us to pretend we were recording the tracks again – for Musician Union rules. Well, frankly, this was never done, and the original master tapes were always used for *TOTP* performances. But a certain MU Representative, 'Doctor Death', as he was famously known back then, would stop by the studio to make sure the track was being re-recorded… We would pretend we were recording the tracks again, all our hits, such as 'Back to the Sixties', 'The Lion Sleeps Tonight' – which had begun as a South African chant, and which the songwriter apparently sold all the rights to, back in 1939, for 10/- (50p)!

"Anyway, at the end of the session, if Doctor Death was satisfied, the engineer would hand him the master tape of the song for the show… All went well with the first three hits and Doctor Death went away with the tapes. But on one occasion it didn't go so well – Doctor Death arrived in a long black coat to witness Brian [Fairweather] and I pretending to do a bass guitar overdub on 'Secret Heart' – well, the bass guitar lead that was supposedly plugged into the amp was just dangling free from my bass, flipping around and hitting Doctor Death's conservative black shoes, while I jumped and danced around and mimed with great enthusiasm! So, alas, we were found out by the ever-watchful Doctor Death and Tight Fit were officially banned from performing on *TOTP* for a certain period of time. To say Clive Calder and Jive records were angry with us is a big understatement. Hence Tight Fit quickly had to have an expensive video made for 'Secret Heart' (filmed in Vienna) to be shown instead of us performing live on the show – Doctor Death had made his terrible mark…!"

Andy Fairweather-Low was another *TOTP* guest with memories of the man from the MU: "'Doctor Death', as he was called, haunted us all. It was his job to witness you recording the backing track of the song that would be used in the show. He would literally stand over you, and you had to play the whole thing too. He was *so* meticulous. But *really*, what a job!"

＊＊＊

The might of the Madchester scene of the mid-80s was probably only exceeded by that of Liverpool at the height of Merseybeat. Down from Manchester they all came: the Smiths, Joy Division, Stone Roses, Happy Mondays, James, 808 State, the Inspiral Carpets (with a young roadie called Noel Gallagher)… And New Order.

For New Order's Peter Hook, his 80s highlight was "appearing on *Top of the Pops* in 1983 – doing that programme was a dream for my generation." But the best-remembered appearance by the four-piece Mancunians, who had arisen from the ashes of Joy Division, came in 1988 when they appeared on *Top of the Pops* to promote 'Blue Monday' – which would become the UK's all-time best-selling 12" single. Determined to boost their indie credibility, at the height of the miming era New Order insisted on playing their hit totally live. It became another legendary *Top of the Pops* moment – though for all the wrong reasons. That reliable chronicler of the Madchester scene, Mick Middles, variously described New Order's live performance as "stunningly poor" or "that dreadful *Top of the Pops* performance."

*David Hamilton, Radio 1 and 2 DJ 1973–86 and the 'Housewives' superstar'
all flared up and raring to go in 1977*

Ed 'Stewpot' Stewart, one of the Radio 1 DJ's who regularly hosted TOTP, surrounded by minis, maxis, hot pants and tank tops... well, it was the 70s!

Nine UK No.1s and 10 further Top 5 hits in just 7 years guaranteed Abba numerous
Top of the Pops *slots*

Scoring No.1 singles in the 70s, 80s and 90s, Blondie were blessed with the supermodel chic of Deborah Harry

During the 1980s, Madness spent more weeks on the UK singles charts than any other group, guaranteeing them regular Top of the Pops *appearances*

She's sung with Jason Donovan, Robbie Williams and Nick Cave, but will remain forever Kylie.
Ms Minogue is snapped here in 2001 at the time of her biggest hit, 'Can't Get You Out Of My Head'

Taking their name from the man whose assassination sparked the First World War, Franz Ferdinand seen here during a 2004 *Top of the Pops* appearance

Top of the Pops Logos

There have been 13 different *Top of the Pops* logos and opening sequences over the show's history and give or take a few minor tweaks, these are the main logos used.

1964-1967

1967-1969

1969-1971

1971-1973

1973-1986

1977

1986-1989

1989-1991

1995-1999

1997

1999-2003

2003-2006

✳ ✳ ✳

On the other side of the pop coin during 1988 were teen sensations Bros. Twins Matt & Luke Goss (and Craig Logan) inspired hysteria on a scale unseen since glam and the Bay City Rollers, a decade before. Bros were symptomatic of pop's late-80s obsession with style over substance, paying at least as much attention to the look as the sound. The group's debut hit 'When Will I Be Famous' certainly reflected the concerns of the period. Bros blazed bright, but brief; scoring eight Top Ten hits over a two-year period. In a 1988 Radio 1 poll, their fans voted 'I Owe You Nothing' the greatest song *ever*. Fittingly, the following year it failed to register at all!

When Soul II Soul were not allowed to sing their No.1 'Back To Life' live on the show, in 1989, leader Jazzie B pulled the group from appearing. But it didn't seem to harm sales, and the record remained at the top for a further five weeks.

It was the 1989 release of 'Could Have Told You So' – a now largely-forgotten single by Halo James that was issued in an incredible 11 separate formats, which led to a new ruling that all singles should henceforth be limited to a maximum of five formats. However, the original strategy worked for Halo James, and 'Could Have Told You So' reached No.6 in February the following year.

And then there were the Smiths... the Beatles for Thatcher's Children – led by the shrewd and knowledgeable S.P. Morrissey.

For Morrissey, the twin platforms of pop legend were *New Musical Express* (which he contributed letters to as a teenager) and *Top of the Pops*: "The most fulfilling thing must be to reach a lot of people, but nowadays the very idea of filling an auditorium has been spat upon by modern groups – but that's just like criticising *Top of the Pops* by people who'll never be on there. *TOTP* is there to be used – we want to reach people."

Scrupulous Smiths-chronicler Johnny Rogan reckons the band's debut promoting 'This Charming Man' in November 1983 "proves one of the highlights of Morrissey's life... For Morrissey, the show represented a crucial epoch. Throughout his adolescence, *Top of the Pops* had been a weekly ritual, its immutable format as permanent and reassuring as the weather forecast... *Top of the Pops* championed and celebrated the true democracy of pop. What other show could house the Beatles alongside Ken Dodd and David Bowie beside Benny Hill without any sense of incongruity?"

'This Charming Man' was probably Morrissey's best-remembered *TOTP* appearance: in control, and careering around with a bunch of gladioli – Dame Edna Lives! Seeing the Smiths on the programme makes for a curious juxtaposition: Morrissey, quiff, in excelsis, in his very element; the bright, glittering, flickering *Top of the Pops* studio lights and Johnny Marr looking every inch the cool rock guitarist…

John Harris later wrote: "Noel [Gallagher's] ambitions were decisively catalyzed by a striking arrival on the weekly TV show that has put a rocket under so many teenage lives: 'When the Smiths came on *Top of the Pops* for the first time, that was it for me… From that day on… I wanted to *be* Johnny Marr.'" And thus, thanks to a 20 year-old BBC institution, was the baton passed down…

With his genuine appreciation of UK pop history, Morrissey remains delighted by every *TOTP* appearance – January 1984 finds the Smiths promoting 'What Difference Does It Make' with Morrissey sporting an old-fashioned hearing aid. He claims it is not an homage to Johnnie Ray, but simply responding to a deaf fan's letter "I thought it would be a nice gesture to wear the hearing aid on *Top of the Pops* to show the fan that deafness shouldn't be some sort of stigma that you try to hide."

Johnny Marr spoke for untold thousands as he recalled the Thursday night ritual. Every week, *Top of the Pops* was preceded by the science show *Tomorrow's World* (and, by the by, what ever *did* happen to all that leisure time we were promised when home computers came in?) "You'd always sit through the last 10 minutes of James Burke," Marr told Ian Gittins, "dying for *TOTP* to come on. It was the primer that you had to go through."

Perhaps the most Madchester edition of *Top of the Pops* came in November 1989 – featuring the Stone Roses, Happy Mondays, 808 State, Electronic and Morrissey.

John Harris watched Ian Brown miming 'Fools Gold' on *Top of the Pops* and later wrote: "Making a mockery of the programme's insistence on miming, he held the microphone way above his head, using it as little more than a prop. His demeanor represented a classic rock gambit: wearing an expression of hard-faced composure, he walked the line between narcissistic cool and outright absurdity." The Roses' rise and fall has been ably and widely chronicled elsewhere, but their 1989 debut album remains a high watermark of UK rock music.

"We should be on *Top of the Pops*," Roses singer Ian Brown stated with typically modest understatement. "I like seeing our record go up and Kylie and Phil Collins go down. There's no point moaning about them. You've got to get in there and stamp them out. Because I believe that we have more worth."

Top of the Pops' 25th anniversary show, on 31 December 1988, saw the return of Jimmy Savile, David Jacobs, Pete Murray, Alan Freeman, Kenny Everett, David Jensen, Tony Blackburn, David Hamilton, Peter Powell and Paul Gambaccini alongside regular presenters Simon Bates, Mark Goodier and Mike Read. But as Steve Wright recalled, it could all have been so very different...

"My abiding memory of that landmark show was getting lost with Tony Blackburn and Noel Edmunds on the 25th Anniversary of the show! We were due to do a link live on the show, and were attempting to find the studio...

"We found ourselves in the building basement at the BBC, and seemed to spend *hours* going along these endless corridors, bumping into lots of men in brown coats mending boilers! We made it with *six* seconds to spare and got properly chewed up by the boss Michael Hurll."

Names from BBC youth TV, like Anthea Turner, Andy Crane and Caron Keating, were also appearing alongside the familiar Radio 1 DJs, in an effort to inject new blood into the long-running institution. But as a tactic to recruit new viewers by appealing directly to the youth audience, it seriously misfired. Among those watching, was the boy who would grow up to be St Etienne's Bob Stanley and he later reminisced to Ian Gittins about what Tony Blackburn called "little blondes from children's programmes": "It was awful. At least you could despise the Radio 1 DJs... Those complete nonentity people made *TOTP* bland and uninteresting. They weren't any good, you didn't care about them and they seemed utterly fake."

After 16 years, the BBC's "other pop show" finally came off air. *The Old Grey Whistle Test* had been BBC2's late-night alternative to BBC1's prime-time *Top of the Pops*. The *Whistle Test* was, from the outset, aimed at an album-buying audience rather than the singles-oriented *Top of the Pops* crowd.

Inevitably, there were crossovers; but if *Top of the Pops* were a family member, it would be a gangly, trendily-dressed teenager; while the *Whistle Test* would be a laid-back, shaggy-haired student in a grubby old greatcoat.

But the late 80s saw the long-running *Pops* facing stiff competition from some cheeky newcomers – *Rapido, The Chart Show, The Roxy, Network 7,*

DEF II, Behind the Beat... Many of the new arrivals were created by Janet Street-Porter, who had been appointed Head of Youth & Entertainment Features at the BBC. It was as if the corporation was aware that the music scene was changing – but couldn't quite catch up with the burgeoning Youth culture.

As it turned out, *Top of the Pops* outlived all those Johnny-come-latelys by a good decade and a half; but after a quarter of a century, the show did seem to be groaning. Unsurprisingly, Band Aid II saw out the 1980s as the UK's No.1. But the burgeoning new technology, acts that were not suited to the television studio, and a creeping sense that pop was reverting to the nursery, all made *TOTP* seem more like a relic than a reflection.

The BBC's Head of Variety Jim Moir, whose association with the programme went back to its very beginning, reflected to Jeff Simpson: "We were conscious that other shows were being created which were making their mark on the public. It became fashionable to say, well, it's 'square', it's not 'cool' to watch *Top of the Pops*."

CHAPTER 4
The 1990s: Shiny, Happy People

Now entering its fourth decade, *Top of the Pops* still maintained its position as the flagship of popular music television. But during the early part of the new decade, the world was busily changing around it. The Berlin Wall was torn down… Nelson Mandela walked free… London burned during Poll Tax riots… Margaret Thatcher was deposed… the "shock and awe" of the first Gulf War was unleashed… And television began to be called "popular culture"…

A single tear helped propel Sinead O'Connor to No.1 in February 1990 with the Prince cover 'Nothing Compares 2 U', deposing the neighbourly Kylie Minogue. The video consisting almost solely of a close-up on the crop-haired singer's face, her pale skin further heightened by the dark background, and the only "action" consisting of that gliding tear!

Queen of the airwaves Madonna was no stranger to controversy (or to its commercial benefits), and her 1990 hit 'Justify My Love' was typical of the controversy she aroused. ("Sex-Rated Madonna" screamed the *Sun*, as MTV banned the video). *Top of the Pops* was more benign, and the Material Girl re-edited the video so that it could be screened on the pre-watershed *Pops*.

This then, was the era of the divas. As well as the indestructible Madonna, Mariah Carey, Celine Dion, Betty Boo, Danii Minogue, Mica Paris, Cathy Dennis, Gloria Estefan, Paula Abdul and Belinda Carlisle were all visitors to the *Top of the Pops* studio during the early 1990s.

While the girls just wanted to have fun (and hits, of course), the summer of 1991 was dominated by one, all-conquering, statistic-shattering, chart-busting, blitzkrieging song… The success of Bryan Adams' '(Everything I Do) I Do It For You' remains, frankly, baffling. While the song is as pleasant as any other big power-ballad of the time, the sheer scale of its success is still inexplicable. Yes, it was the theme from a big summer movie, and yes, Adams had enjoyed UK chart

Oasis mainman, Noel Gallagher, realises a lifetime's ambition by appearing on Top of the Pops

success prior to his mega-hit. But, aside from Alan Rickman's scenery-chewing performance, Kevin Costner's *Robin Hood: Prince Of Thieves* was a pretty mediocre film, and the Adams song was only heard over the end credits. But, despite all that, and being written in a forty-five minute spurt, it remains the most profitable time Bryan Adams ever spent. For an incredible 16 weeks, from July to October, '(Everything I Do) I Do It For You' reigned supreme as the nation's favourite. The song made it into the record books when it even managed to depose Slim Whitman's 1955 'Rose Marie', which had held the record for occupying the No.1 slot for nearly forty years – yodelling Slim had managed a mere 11 weeks.

On 3 October 1991, the 1,439th edition of *Top of the Pops* marked a change of style and emphasis, designed to move the show "radically away from the chart single". BBC mandarins appreciated that something had to be done to reinvigorate the programme, so it was decided to distance the show from the dreary synth pop and one man and a drum machine ethos of the 1980s. The radical new rule now was: if you were on *Top of the Pops*, you sang live!

The programme also moved from central London to the BBC's larger studios at Elstree, which allowed directors more space and flexibility to design how the show looked. Because of the space available *Top of the Pops* now had its own, custom-built studio and, more significantly, its own permanent sound system. It was hoped that this fresh start would give the programme the edge it had so manifestly been lacking.

Stanley Appel had joined the BBC in 1953 as a Probationary Technical Operator following his National Service. "ITV was launched in 1955, and so many BBC staff defected, they made it quite clear that their ambition was to earn £1,000 a year – so that left vacancies at Lime Grove." By 1991 Stan was producing the *Pops* and it was he who supervised the move to Elstree.

To coincide with its move, the following new guidelines were issued for the programme:
1. The No.1 record will always be featured.
2. Any record in the Top Ten will be eligible, even if it was on the show the previous week.
3. The No.2 and 3 will be eligible regardless if they are moving up, down or are static.
4. Records in the 11 – 40 will be considered if they are going up and are good television material.

5. The Top Five in the album charts will be considered.
6. The Top Ten of the US charts will be eligible. Records likely to be featured are those by a British artist.
7. Breakers will be considered from the 11 – 40.
8. In the event of the show not being able to be programmed in the Top 40, then the Top 100 will be considered.
9. Exclusive material not in the charts will also be considered.
10. A record will not get a second showing until it is in the Top Ten.

- It will be most important for the Producer of *Top of the Pops* to have records, videos, lyrics and plans of *any* group available well in advance and all release dates to be known.
- Groups will be encouraged to sing live whenever possible.
- We hope that these changes will help the record industry and make *Top of the Pops* exciting for the audience.

By the summer of 1991, the show's audience figures had dipped to a disastrous 4 million, although they were back up and nudging 8 million as the show relaunched. *Q* magazine's Phil Sutcliffe wrote at the time: "Chart singles are selling far fewer copies and most of them have a narrow appeal within the electro-dance sectors of house, rap and hip-hop which are held to have alienated successive generations of fans who had stuck with the programme, then suddenly experienced that rite of passage out of youth and into something else marked by a sudden observation along the lines of 'Blimey, it must be six months since I last watched *Top of the Pops* – and who the hell are *this* lot?'"

After the relaunch *TOTP* stopped being fixated with the Top 40; there was a loosening of restrictions on the use of promo videos, and the show cast its net wider by allowing star appearances, even if the act didn't currently have a UK chart hit… *Top of the Pops* needed to address itself to a changing pop demographic – but then, 'twas ever thus. By the early 90s however, despite twice the number of singles being released every week, sales were steadily declining, and something new was needed to get back that exciting sense of immediacy.

The insistence on acts singing live, although generally welcomed, did have repercussions. Jeff Simpson listed some "particular stinkers… performed by Bananarama and Danii Minogue." He went on to demonstrate how the singing-live policy backfired: "Many fans didn't want to see their cheery little pop favourites being made fools of, and the record industry didn't appreciate the extra effort involved in turning pop stars into proper live acts. Many acts simply refused to turn up, so *Top of the Pops* was forced to show more and more videos, resulting in the exact opposite to the 'live event' feel the programme was trying to create."

But the programme was also increasingly aware of the stiff competition it was facing. An internal BBC memo read: "Please note that as from 24th August 1992 'exclusive' videos or 'footage' for *Top of the Pops* will only be considered if they are truly 'exclusive'. Any previous showing in the UK by any other broadcaster (ie MTV etc.) will rule the video out of consideration."

However, Assistant Head of Light Entertainment, John Bishop, enthused about the relaunch: "We are building on *Top of the Pops*' strengths – its timing, familiarity and the opportunity to see bands live. New guidelines, which incorporate some existing rules that have ensured the enduring success of the programme, will give producers the flexibility to respond to what's happening in music each week. *Top of the Pops* aims to have its finger firmly on the pulse of the popular music world."

Symptomatic of the big hair and big video budgets of the time, Guns & Roses' nine minute video for 'November Rain' came in at an estimated cost of $1,700,000. It was a big single from the biggest band in the world at the time, but as director Andy Morahan later told *Promo* magazine: "It all became a bit *Spinal Tap* with money!" A UK No.4 in March 1992, for Morahan, the G&R video "marked the end of an era... Soon after that Nirvana happened, and everything became all grungy. Budgets tumbled simply because they could."

You could argue that 20 years after Punk, Grunge became the 90s' defining musical movement. And no one band came to epitomize Grunge more than Nirvana. The first stage-invasion in the history of *Top of the Pops* came in November 1991, when Nirvana were performing 'Smells Like Teen Spirit', and Kurt Cobain was grabbed by an enthusiastic fan. Further invasions followed when over-enthusiastic fans mobbed Backstreet Boys, Symposium, Oasis and Limp Bizkit.

Nirvana's was quite a performance. Upset at having to mime the music, the trio blatantly played around with their instruments – drummer Dave Grohl coming on like Animal on *The Muppet Show*; Krist Novoselic trashed his bass, while Kurt simply did not play his guitar. They became, arguably, the era's defining band; and it is definitely weird watching the clip again now on YouTube, as Nirvana are introduced on the chart rundown, at No.9, sandwiched between Diana Ross and Michael Bolton.

Future anthropologists may well place the first sighting of Britpop as the May 1991 *Top of the Pops*, which saw Blur's appearance to promote their first hit, 'There's No Other Way'. A deeply dippy Damon Albarn remembered the occasion to Stuart Maconie: "It would have been a fantastic experience anyway, but obviously after the E it looked amazing. I just remember before we were on, Vic Reeves, who was in the charts with 'Born Free', was on the other stage and he was doing this big crooner thing and suddenly all this glitter fell from the ceiling and Alex and I were at the side of the stage just looking at each other going: 'Yeah, this is it! Come on!' It was a beautiful moment."

Running parallel to Britpop was the latest teen phenomenon: Take That. The original five-piece line up had been astutely put together by manager Nigel Martin-Smith to mirror the success of US boy band, New Kids On the Block. But Take That soon eclipsed them: becoming the first British group since the Beatles to land four consecutive No.1 singles, and the first act *ever* to have eight singles *enter* the UK charts at No.1.

Take That made their *Top of the Pops* debut in June 1992 – singing live, they performed their cover of the 1986 Tavares hit 'It Only Takes A Minute'. The group observed that their favourite TV pop show seemed in severe danger of running out of steam: "Everybody that worked behind the cameras looked so bored," Robbie Williams told Jeff Simpson. "And I couldn't figure out why they weren't excited to be working at *Top of the Pops* – 'cos I was! Doing your song was like waiting to go in and have your teeth removed."

The *TOTP* rejig did not suit everyone, however. In 1967, "underground DJ" John Peel had called the show "a national disgrace". And when presenting, Peel made no effort to disguise his cynicism. But by 1991 even the curmudgeonly Peel admitted: "I've liked the fact that it had a sort of inescapable integrity. It has been what the title implied, nothing more and nothing less, almost un-riggable, almost impossible to bring new influence to bear. The new format could prove to be an example of the strange instinct people have to stop doing the one thing they do that's actually right."

It was a debate that would continue to rage: were the producers of the programme out of step with what "the kids" wanted? But the answer was always that – good or bad – the show honestly reflected the public's taste... Acts only appeared on the *Pops* because the great British public had visited a record store and bought enough copies of their favourite disc to put it into the charts.

However, the programme's critics argued that it was precisely *because* these acts were on *Top of the Pops* that people kept on going out and buying their records, which, ergo, led to same act appearing on *Top of the Pops*...

The argument was circular and never-ending. But the programme's policy certainly resulted in some intriguing contrasts on the running order during the early 90s... Dame Kiri Te Kanawa on the same show as Carter, The Unstoppable Sex Machine! The bedsit melancholy of Everything But the Girl competing against Daniel O'Donnell. While other shows featured the ubiquitous Robson & Jerome, Nick Cave, Riverdance, Elastica, Andrea Bocelli and, one I'm sure John Prescott was watching, Chumbawumba!

While *Top of the Pops* reigned supreme on BBC1, a competitor sneaked in on BBC2, late one October night in 1992. Yes, it was the show that Robbie Williams later called "*Top of the Pops* with pubes" – *Later...With Jools Holland*. That first *Later...* boasted a soul-heavy line-up of the Neville Brothers, the Christians, Nu Colours and D-Influence. By the end of the first series, Loudon Wainwright III, Television and John Martyn had all been featured performing live. It was certainly a long way from the chart-friendly *Top of the Pops*.

Ironically, the *Top of the Pops* edition of 31 October 1992 saw the incongruous sight of blues veteran John Lee Hooker appearing on the show to perform 'Boom Boom', which got to No.16. The 75 year-old blues maestro Hooker thus claiming the honour of being first OAP to appear live on the programme.

To keep the show's audience interested, performers were sometimes captured live in concert, and bounced back to the *TOTP* studio. Beamed live via satellite from Glasgow, Bruce Springsteen made his *Top of the Pops* debut on 1 April 1993, promoting 'Lucky Town'. Other satellite links included Diana Ross from the Motown Museum, and Bon Jovi from Niagara Falls! April 1994 saw Nicky Campbell introducing Barbra Streisand live on stage at Wembley singing 'As If We Never Said Goodbye' (from *Sunset Boulevard*). Slowly, surely, with stars of that calibre, *Top of the Pops* was becoming an event.

Dick Fiddy, the BFI's TV expert who launched the 'Missing Believed Wiped' search in 1993, explained how it related to *TOTP*: "In the 90s, the charts themselves get devalued... The programme's high watermark was undeniably the 70s – huge-selling singles, and it was self-fulfilling, thousands and thousands of people bought the singles because they'd seen the bands on *Top of the Pops*, it was a win-win situation for the BBC, and the industry.

"By the 90s it had became meaningless, and the ruthless re-invention of music technology meant that the back catalogues of all these bands are in the modern eye, so the charts of today are in competition with the charts of the past 50 years as well! The instantaneous access to the history of pop music means that all modern pop music has to compete with the best of the past.

"*Missing Believed Wiped* began in 1993, we began looking for lost films, but gradually realised there was a lot more TV out there, and a lot of the first things that came back was music television… Seeing Bowie's 'Jean Genie' for the first time in 40 years was extraordinary, but Pink Floyd doing 'See Emily Play', in terrible condition, on *Top of the Pops* … you get the odd 30 seconds, beautiful quality, Syd [Barrett] looking every inch the pop star…"

But despite all the celebrity flag-flying, satellite links and edgy live performances that *Top of the Pops* provided, by the end of 1993 rumours were spreading throughout the BBC that senior management were talking of moving the show from peak-time BBC1 to BBC2, or, even more seriously, considering axing the corporation's weekly pop institution altogether.

Internal BBC memos from the time reveal the parlous state of pop, and the problems faced by *Top of the Pops*: in particular, following the dictate that exclusive screening of videos on the programme meant that they hadn't been seen anywhere else! But looking back, it is hard to believe producers were battling over Haddaway, Joey Lawrence, Therapy, Worlds Apart and Zhane. And was a "Spin Doctors Exclusive" really sending waves of excitement around Elstree? One particularly choice programme from September 1993, balanced Moby, Jazzy Jeff & Fresh Prince (as Will Smith was known in his previous existence), James, Stone Temple Pilots, New Order, Motorhead and Beverley Craven. And – possibly the clincher – where else, but on this uniquely British television institution, would you find Bjork on the same bill as Mr Blobby?

* * *

Brought in from Radio 1, with a brief to prevent the unthinkable, producer Ric Blaxill made a series of seismic changes to *Top of the Pops* when he took over in 1994. A radio veteran, Blaxill had cut his teeth on Chris Tarrant's Capital radio show before moving on to Radio 1, where he helmed Simon Mayo's Breakfast Show for five years. On taking over as *Top of the Pops* producer, Blaxill told *Q* magazine's Tom Doyle: "My mission is simply to get people saying 'God, did you see *Top of the Pops* last night?' again." At the time, there were rumours that the show was to be scrapped. It had hit a low point at the turn of the decade, with the insistence that all acts had to sing live. Fine if you're a traditional rock band, but rather more tricky for an energetic dance act!

Within a year, Blaxill had got the viewing figures up to 8 million plus, introduced celebrity presenters, and commissioned a new theme from Erasure's Vince Clarke. Blaxill also put *TOTP2* on the map, catering to the increasing nostalgia for pop history by mixing vintage clips with highlights from the previous week's show.

Under the headline "Top of the Grandpops", the *Daily Mirror* introduced "the Beeb's new show for the over 30s." Smashie & Nicey style DJs were to be excluded, the feature continued, and BBC2 Controller Michael Jackson promised a show "for people who want to enjoy music from yesterday and for older people who want to catch up with what is happening today. You could say it is an older version of *Top of the Pops*." A *TOTP2* highlight came in May 2001, when Paul McCartney hosted two shows in which he looked back over his career after the Beatles, with clips of Wings and solo appearances over the years.

In March 1994, Mark and Robbie from Take That became the first star presenters of the new era, soon followed by Damon Albarn, Meat Loaf, Kylie Minogue and Jarvis Cocker. In a move which went far beyond irony, Harry Enfield and Paul Whitehouse appeared in character as Smashie & Nicey to present a 1994 edition of *Top of the Pops*. "The bits in between the acts were equally important to get people excited," Blaxill explained. With this in mind, Blaxill went even further, getting TV and sports stars in to present the programme, among them: Jack Dee, Dale Winton, Angus Deayton, Jeremy Clarkson, jockey Frankie Detorri and boxer Chris Eubank. Shurely shome mishtake... the dapper pugilist was called upon to introduce Suggs singing 'Cecilia' at No.6! Then couldn't believe his luck when Sleeper's 'Sale of the Century' was next up...!

Simon Mayo told Phil Sutcliffe how excited he was when invited to present the programme for the first time: "It was fantastic to get on. I'd watched that programme all the time I was growing up and it was incredible being in that studio, thinking of all the bands who'd been there over the past 25 years."

Suddenly, *Top of the Pops* became "cool" again – though not even the persuasive powers of Ric Blaxill and his all-new, re-branded programme could get every act he wanted. Primal Scream famously wouldn't play because of the choice of destination, as Blaxill told Tom Doyle: "'Cry Myself Blind' was No.51, and I adored the song... I was told they were up for doing it and the record company would supply a chartered jet to get them from Dublin at vast expense. But on the day of the show I got a call... saying 'They ain't coming over'. Apparently they wouldn't fly into Luton Airport because it wasn't rock & roll enough for them!" *NME* later understood that the band were worried that if their plane crashed, Primal Scream would be forever associated with the Bedfordshire town. "It's not right, is it? It's not mythical. It's not legendary," moaned the Scream's Bobby Gillespie.

In 1994, Danish singer Whigfield made chart history: 'Saturday Night' became the first new act (and the first female act) ever to debut at No.1 on the UK singles chart. The song managed to do the seemingly impossible because it had been a big hit in European discos that summer and, on returning home, British holiday-makers pushed it straight to the top.

It was an extreme example, but 'Saturday Night' was actually just the latest in a long line of hits which had been hurled up the UK charts by returning holiday makers. During the 1960s few teenagers travelled abroad, but the introduction of cheap package holidays to Europe in the 1970s saw hundreds of thousands of British teenagers soaking up foreign sounds along with the sun and sangria – most notable of those that preceded Whigfield, was Sylvia's 1974 'Y Viva España', while Sabrina's 'Boys' followed in 1988.

Summer novelty it may have been, but 'Saturday Night' gave Whigfield another footnote in chart history: the honour of finally deposing Wet Wet Wet's 'Love Is All Around' (the theme from *Four Weddings & A Funeral*) from the No.1 spot after an incredible 15 weeks at the top. Wet Wet Wet had looked set to finally equal (or even beat) Bryan Adams' 16 week run, until the Wets' record label decided to delete 'Love Is All Around' in an effort to gain momentum for their follow-up. As it happens both 'Everything I Do...' and 'Love Is All Around' were film themes, which may go some way to explaining their chart longevity.

But charming as *Four Weddings & A Funeral* was, and beguiling though the theme was, audiences across the nation couldn't help applauding Jarvis Cocker when the Pulp singer appeared on *Top of the Pops* sporting an "I Hate Wet Wet Wet" T-shirt! Ironic really, that a song that is now cemented into UK chart history was the result of a 20 minute Sunday afternoon writing session back in

1967, while composer Reg Presley was watching Salvation Army group, the Joystrings, on television!

Strangely, the summer of 1995 saw the singles charts make it onto the national news. It was the height of the "Britpop" battle: Blur and Oasis were running pretty much neck and neck in terms of critical plaudits and record sales. And, stoked up by the weekly music press, Blur versus Oasis was keeping the nation entertained. For Noel Gallagher, it was not just a clear north-south divide but also a class one: "working class heroes versus middle class wankers!" The two key singles were released on the same day, but it was Blur who won the battle when 'Country House' (276,000 sales) debuted at No.1, edging ahead of Oasis' 'Roll With It' (218,000).

However, it could be argued that it was the Manchester band who went on to win the war – scoring a further seven No.1 singles. While, ironically, the success of 'Country House' almost did for Blur – guitarist Graham Coxon's distaste was plainly evident in the video. But the chart battle got the entire nation back into a "Who-Will-Be-Top-Of-The-Pops?" frenzy about just which record would be No.1 the following week. Unable to resist a show of triumphalism, Blur bassist Alex James wore an Oasis t-shirt for his band's triumphant *Pops*' appearance.

The subsequent Oasis album, *(What's the Story) Morning Glory*, sold more than 340,000 in its first week; went 12 times platinum; and edged up close to Simply Red and Dire Straits as the UK's best-selling album by a UK act at that time. The album also spawned four hit singles, which once again saw the Gallagher brothers happily installed on *Top of the Pops*. An iconic moment came when, in the tradition of the Who, Noel Gallagher appeared on *Top of the Pops* in February 1996 promoting 'Don't Look Back In Anger', playing a guitar painted like a Union Jack.

Noel loved the show, and used to muck around with the miming element: promoting 'Roll With It', guitarist Noel took over vocal duties from brother Liam – who, in turn, manfully struggled to mime Noel's guitar parts.

In no doubt about the show's importance to him, his brother and his band, Noel enthused to Jeff Simpson: "It's *Top of the Pops* – it's that brand name, it's that logo. It's where I learned to play music. It's where I got the ideas for how bands should be… It's part of your growing up, like riding a bike or playing football. You'll always have a soft spot for *Top of the Pops*. We still say 'How are you feeling? I'm *Top of the Pops*, man!'"

Britpop kept the music press, fans and record buyers all well-happy in the mid-90s. While the battling Gallaghers provided plenty of tabloid fodder, and quotes (of his younger brother Liam, Noel memorably observed: "He's rude, arrogant, intimidating and lazy. He's the angriest man you'll meet. He's like a man with a fork in a world of soup!") But between skirmishes, Noel managed to find time to pen some classic rock & roll singles.

Almost singlehandedly, Oasis had brought the power of pop back into the nation's homes. It was estimated that for Oasis' Knebworth appearance in 1996, one in 24 of the UK population applied for tickets. But it wasn't long before other Britpop contenders, like Powder, Menswear, Echobelly, Sleeper, Denim, Shed Seven, Dodgy and Gene, were all gone with the wind.

By the middle of the decade, many of the big stars were spending more time in the law courts than in the recording studio, with both George Michael and the Stone Roses involved in lengthy and controversial legal battles. And for the BBC, a dramatic and equally controversial move occurred in June 1996 – when, after more than 30 years, *Top of the Pops* moved from Thursday evening to a Friday night slot.

At the time, BBC management promised this was only a temporary, summer move. But, as it turned out, the programme remained locked into Friday nights, where – in a catastrophic blunder – it had to go head to head against *Coronation Street*. With omnibus editions and increasingly fast-paced story lines to introduced to help it combat *EastEnders*, "Corrie" was now regularly pulling in 20 million viewers. Any programme facing such stiff competition would get massacred – and *Top of the Pops* was no exception.

The record industry was appalled by the BBC's decision, with a number of music company executives threatening to withdraw their support for the long-running show. A typical response at the time came from EMI's marketing manager, Richard Grafton, who complained: "*Top of the Pops* moving is the worst thing, it's simply the wrong day."

"Moving *Top of the Pops* from a Thursday to a Friday night has changed the whole way British music is sold," Pete Waterman fulminated to Jeff Simpson. "No matter what the BBC thinks, it ain't the same."

In hindsight, it was clearly a disastrous move; but at the time, you could understand the reasons for decision. By having *Top of the Pops* broadcast early evening on a Friday, it meant that viewers could go straight out to the shops the following morning and buy the songs they had seen and heard. The Saturday morning sweep for a hit single back in the 1990s could have meant a trawl around high street branches of Woolworth's, WH Smith, Our Price, Virgin and HMV!

But it was not just the change of day for *TOTP*, the very nature of the music – and the way music was seen – had altered. With the explosion of dance had come the cult of the DJ, and the sight of a bloke – and it usually was a chap – standing behind a record deck, dubbing and scratching, did not make for great television.

And so, for *Top of the Pops*, as the 90s progressed, the problems remained; in a 2006 feature for *The Word*, former BBC mandarin Trevor Dann pinpointed the problems: "Blaxill was thwarted by three things out of his control. Firstly, the singles chart had lost any meaning as a mechanic to drive the show. Records simply never went up: they entered at the highest point… then gradually fell. Secondly, in 1996, the BBC realised that the show could never compete with the powerful soaps… and decided to move the show to Friday nights where its failure would be less conspicuous… and thirdly, with the new Top 40 now revealed by Radio 1 on a Sunday instead of a Tuesday, *TOTP* was permanently five days late with the news."

While battling the BBC, Ric Blaxill was at least blessed with the continuing power of Britpop, and the arrival of another pop phenomenon. Undeniably, the single most important pop sensation of 1996 was the Spice Girls… For only the fifth time ever, each of the group's first three singles reached No.1, meaning that they held the top spot for a grand total of 12 weeks during the year. It also meant that the Spice Girls virtually lived in the *Top of the Pops* studio. 'Wannabe' reached No.1 in 31 countries around the world, proclaiming the arrival of Girl Power wherever it went. It was a 1996 feature for the newly-launched *Top of the Pops* magazine that first gave the five girls their aliases – Ginger, Posh, Sporty, Baby and Scary. And, echoing Pete Townshend's jacket and Noel Gallagher's guitar, Geri Halliwell sported a Union Jack dress at the 1997 Brit Awards.

But the year that brought the girls together, also saw the boys part, when Take That split, and Robbie Williams launched his solo career. Nobody, but nobody, would have placed a bet on it being "the fat one from Take That" that went on to solo success, so it was with particular relish that Robbie watched as his solo career eclipsed that – not only of his former band mates – but pretty well everyone else in the UK pop firmament.

Well, who'd have thought it? Record-breaking holder of more Brit awards than any other artist… Record breaking crowds at Knebworth… Record-breaking £80 million deal with EMI… Robbie made his solo debut on *Top of the Pops* in August 1996, when the guest presenter was Peter Andre. Robbie ensured that his every *Top of the Pops* appearance was memorable – although dropping his trousers Brian Rix-style to reveal tiger underpants did little to enhance his artistic standing.

The BBC was celebrating its 60th year of broadcasting, and despite the switch to Fridays *Top of the Pops* still reigned supreme, seeing off the competition once again, when Channel 4's *The White Room* was axed in 1996. More TV music arrived in 1996, when Chris Evans launched *TFI Friday*… And 1996 was also the year that saw pop scamp Jarvis Cocker invade the stage during The Brits' broadcast of Michael Jackson's 'Earth Song'. Pulp now battled Oasis as most talked-about band, winning the Mercury Prize for *Different Class*, and running into controversy with 'Sorted For E's & Wizz'. Promoting the song on *Top of the Pops*, Jarvis Cocker waved a copy of the *Daily Mirror* which denounced the single in banner headlines!

After three years at the helm, during which time he gave the programme back some of its gravitas, despite being undermined by the switch to Friday nights, Ric Blaxill left – to be replaced by producer and occasional programme director, Chris Cowey. On his watch, DJs Zoe Ball, Jayne Middlemiss and Jo Whiley were introduced as regular presenters.

Another presenter who was delighted to be there was Radio 1 DJ Mark Radcliffe. Like so many other viewers, growing up in Bolton he had waited impatiently for that precious 30 minute show on a Thursday night: "It was like a beacon of light. I know it's a cliché, but everything *seemed* very black and white back then, until the light was let in by the mirrors reflecting off Noddy Holder's top-hat!

"*Top of the Pops* provided a portal into another, brighter world. You didn't get to see live bands in Bolton unless you went to the Technical College, and I was too young... So if I wanted to see Status Quo doing 'Down Down', you watched *Top of the Pops*. You had, of course, copied down the chart rundown from Radio 1 on Tuesday, and Thursday you watched to see who was on. I even used to record it on my reel-to-reel, but of course you couldn't edit out the stuff you didn't like – and my gran always seemed to be talking in the background!

"Let's be frank, the show also had a hand in the awakening of sexuality, I mean, forget the record, but Pan's People, five girls dancing around in their knickers, well *that* certainly provided a glimpse into another world!

"So of course I was absolutely delighted to be asked to present the programme in 1997. Anyone who was a DJ – and this included John Peel – was delighted; it was almost a status symbol, a confirmation that you had made it. Marc Riley and I were doing the Radio 1 *Breakfast Show* when we were first asked on. We were thrilled, but it meant a car from Manchester to Elstree, and we were absolutely *knackered*. Back to bed by 2am and up again at 4.30… We knew millions were watching us, because the Spice Girls were on. Me and Marc were, I suppose, slightly ironic – trying to deconstruct the whole thing, but then we took that attitude to everything.

"I think for our first appearance, we borrowed suits from Paul Smith in Manchester. The second time, in May 1997, we wore white shirts, which left us looking like waiters at a slightly down-at-heel trattoria. Who did we introduce…? Placebo, Skunk Anansie, Katrina & the Waves… A rather hysterical, quick you might miss 'em element, was apparent in our presentation – perhaps we were trying to comment on the transient nature of pop. I just remember being really thrilled, but looking and acting absolutely terrified!

"I was really proud to have done it before it disappeared, the downfall was moving it away from a chart-based show, and the music, some bloke in an anorak with a record player…! But Marc and I *were* responsible for that great *Sun* headline 'Too Ugly For *Top of the Pops*?' There seemed to be a consensus that the programme would look better if it was presented by someone more photogenic... like Fearne Cotton. They asked me what I thought and I said that even *I* thought Fearne Cotton made for a more attractive presenter…!"

* * *

In the end, and for all the wrong reasons, *the* song of 1997 was Elton John's reworking of his own 'Candle in the Wind'. Rewritten hastily in memory of Princess Diana, 'Candle in the Wind '97' proved to be the last record George Martin would produce, and went on to become the best-selling single of all time, eclipsing even 'White Christmas'. Surprisingly though, it was only No.1 in the UK for just over a month.

Top of the Pops went global the following year, when the BBC announced it had plans for a German edition of the programme. The brand was eventually licensed by the BBC to nearly 20 European countries. The idea being that each territory would feature their own popular acts on a *Top of the Pops* set, but that to bolster the show's appeal, they could also "poach" whichever global acts were currently gracing the UK's *Top of the Pops*. Thus, Italy or Spain or Holland could promote its own home-grown talent, as well as featuring U2 or the Spice Girls or Jennifer Lopez when they made appearances on the show in London.

It was a successful ploy by BBC Worldwide, and the *Top of the Pops* brand was, by the end of the 20th Century, one of the most recognised in pop, with an estimated 100 million viewers across 90 countries. To maintain the brand's integrity, a lot of hard work had to be put in to match each country's presentation with that of its parent: it was considered essential that every licensed edition had the same recognizable *Top of the Pops* set, logo and style.

Unsurprisingly, artist management companies and record labels were delighted with this roll-out, and keen to work on the new global *Top of the Pops*. It meant that as a single peaked, one appearance by a megastar like Madonna could be re-shown on shows in individual territories, making it seem as if Madonna (for example) had found time in her busy schedule to pop along to *TOTP* in Turin, Amsterdam, Frankfurt, and the rest... It was like the good old days of promotional videos, allowing an artist to appear to be in more than one place at the same time.

Steve Wright remembered: "The show was *so* huge globally too. Even big international stars were in awe. One day Donna Summer was performing, and she took me to one side to confide that she was trembling and nervous. 'But,' as I pointed out, '*you* are Donna Summer!' 'Yes', she replied.. 'But *this* is *Top of the Pops*!'

"*Top of the Pops* is a Force Of Nature ... It's the London Palladium of pop ... and never forget the show is not about the presenters, or even the bands – it is all about the *show*!"

As for the competition... *The Chart Show* was axed in 1998 after 12 years, but in the late 1990s pop on TV was in pretty buoyant shape. As well as *Top of the Pops*, Channel 5 began *The Pepsi Chart* and MTV and VH-1 were on air throughout the day, and night, seven days a week.

But there it still was! Just open 1998's festive edition of *Radio Times*... And the centrepiece of Christmas Day's viewing – as much a part of the festive fare as roast turkey, fused fairy lights and Advocaat – was *Top of the Pops* at 12.50pm.

Sitting pretty, that particular year, between the film of *Miracle On 34th Street* and a repeat of the *Morecambe & Wise Show*, followed by that other much-loved national institution: The Queen at 3pm.

* * *

In 1998, the list of the UK's best-selling albums of all time still included the soundtrack from 1965's *The Sound of Music*, *South Pacific* and *The Black & White Minstrel Show*. The singles charts, as ever, told a different story... In the UK, the 700th No.1 had come in 1994 with Chaka Demus & Pliers' 'Twist & Shout'; the 800th was All Saints' 'Bootie Call' in 1998.

But the female who most mesmerised *Top of the Pops* audiences that year was Cher, returning to the programme an incredible 33 years after she had first appeared. Back then it had been in full hippie mode with husband Sonny; but in October 1998 she was back on the show – this time triumphantly alone and performing her biggest hit, 'Believe'. A UK No.1 for seven weeks, 'Believe' went on to beat Madonna, Celine Dion, Cilla Black etc. to become the UK's highest-selling single by a female artist to date.

The following year, Boyzone enjoyed their fourth No.1 album with *By Request*. It sold 329,000 copies in its first week, more than the rest of the Top Twenty UK album chart put together! They created the template for the successful boy bands that followed, notching up 16 consecutive Top Five singles, including six No.1s. Right up there alongside them – and indeed, right up there in terms of *Top of the Pops* incongruity – was the venerable composer Andrew Lloyd Webber accompanying Boyzone on the programme as they performed his 'No Matter What' from 1998's *Whistle Down the Wind*.

The honour of the final No.1 – not just of the decade, but of the millennium – went to another boy band, Westlife. The double A-sides were both covers: one of Abba's 'I Have A Dream' and the other of Terry Jacks' 1974 'Seasons in the Sun'. Abba had been denied the top spot with their song in 1979 by Pink Floyd, but now Westlife became the first act since Elvis Presley back in 1962 to have four No.1s in a single year. And that was only the beginning...

Westlife had started out under the watchful eye of Boyzone singer Ronan Keating, manager Louis Walsh, and an ambitious record company executive called Simon Cowell. With such high-octane backing, no wonder that Westlife became the most successful singles act of the 21st Century. By the time they called it a day in 2011, the Irish quintet had scored an astonishing *fourteen* UK No.1 singles! They had also made UK chart history, eclipsing even the Beatles (and Oasis, Steps, Boyzone…) by having every one of their first seven singles *enter* the charts at No.1. Westlife also dallied with pop aristocracy, recording with Mariah Carey and Diana Ross. The scale of their success ensured that every *Top of the Pops* appearance during the group's 12 year career generated fan frenzy.

Such is the fragile nature of pop stardom, however, that for every Boyzone, there is also a slew of acts who are hardly remembered outside of immediate family; step forward Adam Rickitt; A1, Bran Van 3000, Mario Piu, Mr Oizo, Sixpence None the Richer, Hepburn… This final year of the century was also the one that saw the Spice Girls launch their solo careers; and, a further reminder of the power of TV soaps on the pop charts, *EastEnders'* Martine McCutcheon launched her singing career with a No.1, 'Perfect Moment'.

It is worth briefly reflecting on the musical differences between the UK and USA during the 1990s: in the UK Oasis, Robson & Jerome and Simply Red held sway; while in America, three of the Top Ten best-selling albums of the decade were by Garth Brooks!

For all the mutinous rumblings and troubled waters, the Good Ship Pop sailed serenely on, and the record industry saw no reason why things should not continue as they had during the preceding four decades. The record companies would continue to invest in new music, throwing enough mud at the wall in the hope that some of it would stick. Fans would then buy the product of those successful acts from a record store, generating sufficient sales to propel their single into the chart, which would then result in a *Top of the Pops* appearance, thereby generating more sales, further hits and, with a bit of luck, a career… It had worked well enough since Lonnie Donegan launched the skiffle boom in the mid-1950s; it had worked well enough since *TOTP* was launched in 1964. Indeed, the show had already outlived disco, glam, punk, the new romantics and house… In tandem with the record industry, everything remained, as Vivian Stanshall once wrote: "changing and changeless as canal water."

But late in 1998, without any noticeable warning, everything suddenly changed, when Shawn Fanning – a 19 year-old from Massachusetts – launched something called Napster on something called the Internet…

CHAPTER 5
The 21st Century: I Predict a Riot

In short, it all began (or, for *TOTP*, ended) with compression. For once sound could be stored digitally (the code we now know as MP3) the entire world, or as it came to be better known, the entire worldwide web was your oyster.

But where Napster (named after Fanning's "nappy" hairstyle) really scored was its speed. Pre-Fanning, finding your favourite song in the murky world of cyberspace was incredibly time-consuming. Record companies had been slow off the mark making their song catalogues available, but Fanning's software speeded up the process, as if by magic. Napster also stole a march on the rest by the simply telling visitors to the site what files everyone else had! Thus the files containing your favourite music ("Hey dad, you want every song the Beatles ever recorded – for free?"), anywhere in the world, could be transferred across cyberspace, from hard drive to hard drive. Within two years, Napster was being visited regularly by up to 100 million users.

The 21st Century had begun with dire warnings, even before anyone had heard of Napster. According to the doom merchants – and quite a lot of experts who really should have known better – at the stroke of midnight on 31 December 1999, the world as we knew it would end with the Y2K bug turning computers across the globe into useless lumps of pale grey plastic. And as *everything* was now run by computers it would be, in the words of REM, "the end of the world as we know it…" As it happened, the computer experts cashed in, but nothing actually happened… The world continued to spin; pin numbers continued to work; telephone exchanges carried on connecting numbers; computers recognised there had been a year change. A century change. A millennium change. And I feel fine…

A typically restrained Lady Gaga (Stefani Joanne Angelina Germanotta) performing on a
Top of the Pops *Christmas special*

With disaster averted, it was Manic Street Preachers who pointed the way to the new pop millennium, when 'The Masses Against the Classes' became the first No.1 of the new century. Released, and impishly deleted, on the same day, the Manics' Nicky Wire had begged the 50,000 strong crowd at the band's 1999 New Year's Eve show in Cardiff to buy it, thereby guaranteeing the removal of Westlife from the top of the charts!

The Manics were no strangers to controversy. In 1994, they had appeared on *Top of the Pops* to promote 'Faster', wearing terrorist style balaclavas. Unsurprisingly, complaints had flooded in. But rather than cheap publicity stunts, their calculated rebellion was seen as a direct response to the fabricated pop that was swamping the charts – at a time when chart placings still mattered.

The year 2000 began slowly, as was customary, with the post-Christmas hangover period when the credit card bills started to arrive. The *TOTP* studio welcomed Coldplay, whose first hit 'Yellow' reached No.4 in mid-2000. It was also a year which saw Ronan Keating launch a solo career, as did Spice Girls Melanie C and Mel B (a year behind Geri Halliwell). Meanwhile, Daft Punk were enthusiastically received by the *TOTP* audience when they performed their huge club hit 'One More Time', which peaked at No.2 just prior to Christmas 2000.

Diva appearances were no longer restricted to the ladies in the new century, as Prince proved when he insisted that the backstage area be cleared, just when Robbie Williams wanted to chill out. Later, appearing live on the show, the Robster told the studio audience: "Tonight I'm going to kick somebody's head in like it's 1999!" No stranger to controversy, Robbie's summer 2000 appearance promoting 'Rock DJ' also resulted in a spontaneous Shock! Horror! moment – when his trouser-dropping incident, live on air, prompted 150 complaints to the BBC.

It was all good farcical fun, but the UK record industry was no longer laughing. They had been laughably slow in waking up to the threat posed by Napster and the internet; now suddenly they realised that "the kids" had little need for physical product. They didn't have to rely on the opinions of critics, and they had even less use for radio and TV turning them on to new music… Who wanted to wade through, like, crap, to hear or see what other, like, *old* people thought *you* wanted.

Suddenly, everything was there just for the asking, right in front of you, twenty-four seven. All thanks to a tiny silicon chip: if your mate heard a song they liked, there was always another nerdy mate who could access that music on their computer and pass it on to you. In one short step, the entire record industry and music media became virtually redundant.

Writing in *The Word* in 2010, Andrew Harrison looked back: "At a record company meeting in 2000, an executive demonstrated how simple it was to download a tune by one of their artists. After a minute or so of silence someone spoke up: 'We're fucked!'" (In the face of declining sales, sadly *The Word* itself also went belly-up in 2012.)

* * *

Still, *TOTP* soldiered on, and among the acts making their debuts on the programme during 2000, were indie darlings Belle & Sebastian, Muse, Pink, and, er, Bob the Builder. That year also brought a timely reminder of the enduring power of the pop video, with Kylie Minogue's No.1 'Spinning Around' – the first No.1 for the "new look" Kylie. Gone for good was the big-haired soap star and PWL puppet – and all thanks to a tiny pair of gold pants! Kylie's second chart-topper of the new decade, 2001's 'Can't Get You Out Of My Head' was propelled by Dawn Shadforth's promo, which the director memorably described as "Rio meets Basildon in a future Kylie universe".

Kylie's success displayed true star power, and proved that a striking video could still help propel a song into the charts. Ironically, the promo that has been called "perhaps the greatest video ever" – and voted the No.1 of all time in a 2004 *Q* magazine poll – was for a song which was only ever a modest hit. Immeasurably poignant, Johnny Cash's 2003 'Hurt' featured a gaunt, clearly dying, Man in Black looking at photos and film of his life as it flashed before him, on screen – just six months later, Cash was gone.

On a jauntier note, 21st Century pure pop meant plenty of *Top of the Pops* appearances by Atomic Kitten, Five, Steps, SClub7, All Saints, Louise, Blue and Hear'Say – and a nation were united (in grief?) when Steps announced their split on Boxing Day 2001. A more sombre note was struck with another departure in November 2001 – when, just a day after his death, *Top of the Pops* broadcast a special tribute to George Harrison, featuring footage of him in and out of the Beatles.

* * *

In a cheeky riposte to the increasing homogenization of the pop industry, and its reliance on promotional videos, Blur's Damon Albarn and cartoonist Jamie

Hewlitt's 2001 creation, Gorillaz, became the first non-human group to make their *TOTP* debut since – what – the Archies…?

And if you thought that One-Hit Wonders were just a thing of the 70s: remember Gordon Haskell? His 'How Wonderful You Are' (the most requested song in the history of Radio 2) was only kept off the Christmas No.1 by the combined power of Robbie Williams & Nicole Kidman. What makes the Haskell hit even more noteworthy is that it marked a rare *Top of the Pops* appearance by a former member of prog-rock Gods, King Crimson! (*Interesting, but not strictly relevant footnote: both Bryan Ferry and Elton John had in their time auditioned for a place in the court of the Crimson King).

Among the acts who made their first *TOTP* appearances in 2001 were Starsailor, Elbow, Dido and Daniel Bedingfield. Travis also made their debut and – with true rock & roll abandon – had a custard pie fight on air. But the old-guard fought back on 19 October 2001, when U2 – riding high as the world's biggest band – appeared live to help launch the new-look *Top of the Pops*.

Producer Chris Cowey was not alone in being unhappy when the show was booted out of the BBC's Elstree studios to make more room for the four days a week *EastEnders*. For many of the bands, a visit to the adjacent Albert Square had been de rigueur – Travis, the Wedding Present, the Bluetones and Black Box Recorder were just some of those who made the pilgrimage to Walford

Though briefly re-located to the Riverside studios in Hammersmith, *Top of the Pops* soon made it back to its spiritual home at Television Centre. Cowey had fought for a bigger permanent studio and insisted on a celebrity backstage area where acts could be seen relaxing after a performance.

It was an astute move: *Heat* magazine had launched a few years before, unleashing a torrent of imitators, all of which wallowed in the UK's booming celebrity culture. "Exclusives" were promised and fought over – though "exclusive" no longer had *quite* the same meaning. *Top of the Pops* was still capable of attracting the biggest names in music, and glimpses of the stars caught chilling out after the show only added to the its lustre.

But there was still plenty of megastar-madness that you didn't get to see – onscreen, or in the celebrity mags. Arriving to promote her 2001 hit 'My Love Don't Cost a Thing', Jennifer Lopez immediately seized the record for the largest entourage ever witnessed in the entire history on *Top of the Pops*. Jenny-from-the-block brought no fewer than 60 (sixty!) helpers in her wake – including three chefs. And before her arrival, all 10 dressing rooms had been redecorated and rounded off with a fresh orchid in each. Poor old R. Kelly had to make do with a mere 43 minders. While Whitney Houston's "people" declined the best dressing room the BBC had to offer because: "Whitney doesn't do stairs."

It was all a mighty long way from the 70s, when music industry insider David Stark, having blagged his way backstage to the show, found himself helping Abba's Agnetha to find a socket for her hairdryer – because there was nobody else around to help!

The 21st Century saw *Top of the Pops'* declining Friday night audience compounded by the launch of *Pop Idol* in 2002 and *The X Factor* in 2004. It was what David Bowie called: "the cruise ship entertainment aspect of British rock"; though for the *Pops*, it was more like a shipwreck... And by then it was too late.

With entire channels now devoted to pop music; celebrities preferring the cosy chat-show sofa; and audiences able to access their favourites directly via their websites or blogs the writing was clearly on the wall. And in the end, despite the increasingly youthful and "edgy" presenters, and even despite Victoria Beckham graciously appearing to promote her as yet unreleased single, *Top of the Pops* just began to look like a bit of a relic.

As audiences grew and grew for the phone-in TV talent shows, such as *Pop Idol* and *The X Factor*, it became clear that the end was nigh. There was a rather pointless immediacy to entertainment in the 21st Century, with nobody prepared to wait for exclusives or sneak previews... *Everything* – good, bad or indifferent – had to be available *now*! And it was not just *Top of the Pops* that was suffering.

The entire music industry seemed unprepared for the onslaught: Apple launched iTunes in 2003; MySpace soon followed; Facebook, 2004; YouTube, 2005; Twitter, 2006... And as the industry bible *Music Week* wrote in 2009, reflecting on the changes the industry had seen during the first decade of the new century: "For the first time, bands in the noughties could interact with their fans with an immediacy and intimacy that would have shocked previous generations. No longer would the public have to wait by their radios [and TVs] in the vain hope of hearing the latest effort from their musical heroes – now, within the space of a few clicks, they could hear it, download it and talk about it – quite possibly even share it."

Even the industry itself appeared to have been overwhelmed by the changes. Talking to Miranda Sawyer in 2008, Sony BMG's Ged Doherty said: "Just five years ago, you'd release a handful of products from every album, meaning three singles, a couple of 12" mixes. Maybe up to ten. Now for the last Justin Timberlake album (2006's *FutureSex/LoveSounds*) we released 181 products! And 140 of them were digital: ringtones, wallpaper, soundtracks for games."

Fans could now rip, mix and burn on a whim, and digital copying meant that copies could be pressed at home, with sound quality as professional as a recording studio's. Though not all the new technology triumphed: at Christmas 2002, for example, Robbie Williams' *Life Thru a Lens* sold precisely seven copies on Mini Disc!

In the last years of its life *Top of the Pops* patently struggled to stay afloat, given the immediacy of all the new technology and the multiplicity of fresh platforms available. Combined UK single sales were now in excess of 50 million, suggesting that there was still a strong audience for pop music in the new decade. But, during 2001 alone, more than 7,000 singles were released; at best, in the course of a year, the show could feature less than 500. In 2002, leading up to its 2000th show, the show continued to demonstrate its eclecticism, with performances from Mercury Prize-winning Ms Dynamite, Moby, Supergrass, Beverly Knight, Coldplay and Busted.

Top of the Pops 2, meanwhile, had a hand in effectively launching the career of the late Eva Cassidy, when they played her version of 'Over the Rainbow', which led to the posthumous *Songbird* reaching No.1 on the UK album charts. And BBC Scotland, anxious not to be left behind, immortalised Madonna, Eminem and Geri Halliwell in the mercifully short-lived *Top of the Poppets*!

On into the new century, and the TV bandwagon rolls on and on… Will Young and Gareth Gates smash sales records on the back of their *Pop Idol* appearances, with Gareth alone racking up three No.1 singles during 2002. Such "picked by the public" pop stars topped the charts for 18 weeks during the year, selling nearly 7 million singles. All sales undeniably bolstered and boosted by *Top of the Pops* appearances, but the BBC show was seen to be struggling in the face of strong competition from the all-conquering phone-in shows.

The sea-change in chart music was further proof of the power of direct access TV, which meant a viewer's phone call could make all the difference – directly, and immediately, affecting an act's future. There was a weary sense of 'why bother to wait for half an hour on a weekday night to see what was No.1 when with one phone call on Saturday, the result was in your own hands'. The votes dictated the show's winner and then – even if only a small percentage of the TV audience bought the winner's record – it was virtually guaranteed the No.1 spot.

As singles continued to burn-out as quickly as they rose, the titanic struggle to reach the top was largely a thing of the past. A No.1 hit now owed more to hype, marketing and telephone voting than talent or musical ability. There was no slow slog, climbing like in the good old days of Gerry & the Pacemakers, Slade or the Jam. During 2002, for example, 40 singles took it in turn to occupy the No.1 slot. And in December 2002, Girls Aloud exploded out of the TV talent show *Popstars: The Rivals,* hitting No.1 with their debut 'Sound of the Underground'…

For that all-important 2000th edition of *Top of the Pops* in September 2002… "From Beatles to Kittens, we've brought you seven hundred and seventy-six number ones on two thousand shows. It is the biggest music show in the world. It's still number one, it's *Top of the Pops*!" enthused presenter Jamie Theakston, introducing N-Trance, Tom Jones & Wyclef Jean, Jurgen Vries, White Stripes, Appleton and Atomic Kitten. Status Quo rocked all over the world (again), well on their way to becoming the group who racked up more *Top of the Pops* appearances than any other – an amazing 86 times over the thirty-seven years between 1968 and 2005!

Still going strong into the 21st Century, and with the vintage Status Quo four-man line up back together again, Francis Rossi reflected: "Doing *Top of the Pops* was like a day-off for Quo! It was such a joy, so relaxing – and we *knew* it was selling our records into the bargain! Despite everyone thinking that we raised hell and it was a drink orgy … we got as dangerous as always having a curry on the day. Very orderly.

"It was an interesting barometer for bands like us too. We once heard 'Yellow River' by Christie on Radio 1, and thought we would check them out on the *Pops*. Once we had seen how clean cut they were, we knew that we had to rough up our image a little. After all we were rock & roll!

"Quo are the only re-formed band that nobody is dead in. Our first appearance with 'Matchstick Men' in '68, we could not *believe* we were on the show, along with the likes of Dave Dee etc. and those lovely blokes the Tremeloes. They all became mates.

"When you saw artists looking up whilst performing – they were of course staring at the monitors above, but it has to be said that it wasn't all vanity… it was actually people not *believing* they were on the show. It was like a 'pinch me' moment. One exception was Marc Bolan… When Marc stared at the monitor he was checking out his look – and if you recall the way he shook his curly hair as he stared up? Well he was actually preening himself. Bless him.

"When we walked onto that set in '68 we all thought we had better enjoy it as we had maybe five years left in the business.. We thought 'Let's soak this up… it's never going to last'… Little did we know that 100 shows later we would not only be still going, but greedier than ever for more! *Top of the Pops* helped shape our careers and bands like us owe a never-ending debt to the show that reflected the hits of the day and made stars into superstars."

✳ ✳ ✳

The critics were busy championing the three Rs back in 2002: rap, R&B and rock. And though the *Pops* audience were still enjoying Blue, Robbie Williams, Sugababes, Oasis, Girls Aloud and Liberty X, these acts were just not convincing US audiences – and for the first time since 1963, there were no British acts in the American Hot 100.

Even in 2002 though, it was not exclusively newcomers on the show, nor exclusively living artists. Elvis Presley returned from beyond the grave, to top the UK charts with the remixed 'A Little Less Conversation' – giving him his 18th chart topper, and crucially pushing him just ahead of the Beatles. The King remained at No.1 for four weeks, and would probably have stayed there longer, had the record label not deleted the single to allow for more promotion of the new Gareth Gates single.

The Rolling Stones too were still going strong, as they celebrated their 40th anniversary. And to prove it, their *Licks* tour managed to become the second highest-grossing tour in the history of rock & roll – oh, and the one that beat them: the most successful ever? Well, that was the Stones' own *Voodoo Lounge* dates in 1994/6.

On a slightly less elevated scale, but in a rather touching display of fan loyalty, John Otway encouraged his faithful followers to propel his 'Bunsen Burner' into the Top Ten in 2002, which resulted in the manic Otway returning to *of the Pops* for the first time since 1977. Bless him, Otway embraces his wilful, own-goal philosophy: his *own* website even acknowledges him as Rock & Roll's Greatest Failure! But there is much joy to be found in watching Otway perform on *TOTP* during the 70s: he is visibly delighted at being on the show performing 'Really

Free'; proves manifestly incapable of miming; and concludes by balancing precariously on an amplifier to the evident bafflement of an audience who had really rather hoped to see the Brotherhood Of Man instead!

Cult hero Otway still holds the record for the longest gap between *TOTP* appearances (25 years!), and admits that his yearning for fame the second time around didn't merely revolve around the charts: "We didn't *just* want another hit, we wanted to be back on the show more than anything!

"It was a gauge as to just how famous you were. I recall a cab driver asking me one day what I did, and I proudly with tongue in cheek replied that I was a pop star. Gaping at me through the mirror, you could see he was having trouble working me out, 'ere', he said, 'have you been on *Top of the Pops* then, mate?'

'Well, yes, a couple of time actually,' I replied. And that was enough to convince him that I was indeed a star. Not just a recording act, but a *true star* – and I was treated like royalty for the rest of the journey!

"I also wanted 'Bunsen Burner' to be big – we had proved we could circumvent the chart process by utilising our fan-base to the maximum effect. And in our band was a young bass player called Seymour – and I *knew* it would be his only chance to ever appear on the show, which he duly did.

"With 'Really Free' I had been driven to the BBC in a record company limo – but with 'Burner' I rode there on my bike!

"I was convinced that I would be out of place and that no-one would know me, but as I was passing through the reception area a voice rang out 'Oi… Otway!' It was Badly Drawn Boy, which made me feel welcome once again! We actually performed the song three times on the day and each time the crowd got more and more bonkers. We had a great, *great* day.

"The first time I did the show I was convinced I would be back on it really soon, so I bought a bottle of champagne to open when it happened. It lasted five years – I got thirsty; but it took 25!"

* * *

Eventually, it got to a point where – with all the phone-in hits and acts entering and vanishing in the blink of an eye – no one really seemed to care what was in the fondly-remembered Hit Parade. Around 2003, Bill Bailey sagely observed: "There's more evil in the charts than in an Al Qaeda suggestion box!"

It was that same year that Chris Cowey left the show, and children's' TV presenter Andi Peters was brought in to breathe life into the moribund *Pops*. But he was on slippery ground... The decline continued unabated, and not just audiences for the show, but throughout the music industry, with 2003's UK singles sales down nearly 30% on the previous year.

As the programme limped towards its inevitable demise, there were still occasional highlights; and it has to be said that teen idol Justin Timberlake joining left-field art-rockers the Flaming Lips in 2003 was one of them! Bopping in the background, dressed up – as what looked, to the uninformed eye, like a dolphin – Justin gamely perseveres, as the Lips' Wayne Coyne has fun urging the *TOTP* audience to sing along to their Top Twenty hit 'Yoshimi Battles the Pink Robots Pt.1'!

On 28 November 2003, the show saw one of the most radical overhauls in its history – in what was widely reported as a make-or-break attempt to revitalise the long-running series. In a departure from the previous format, the show played more up-and-coming tracks ahead of any chart success, and also featured interviews with artists. The launch show – which was live, and an hour long – was notable for a performance of 'Flip Reverse' by Blazin' Squad, which featured hordes of hooded teenagers choreographed to dance around the outside of Television Centre. Despite serious concerns about the end of civilisation as we knew it, the TV Centre, and *Top of the Pops*, survived.

One of the biggest-hitting presenters on that new-look *TOTP* was Victoria Beckham, who greeted the ubiquitous Westlife, as well as Mis-Teeq, Will Young, Kylie Minogue and Gareth Gates. Other acts who made their debut during 2003 included the homegrown Dizzee Rascal and *American Idol* winner, Kelly Clarkson. *Pop Idol* winner Michelle McManus also managed to reach No.1 with her debut single after winning the 2003 show, but was dropped by her label soon after.

Some traditions remained in place however. In 2003 the Darkness did a *TOTP* turn to promote 'Christmas Time (Don't Let the Bells End)' which brought back fond memories of Wizzard in excelsis.

In January 2004, *Top of the Pops* celebrated its 40th anniversary. After notching up four decades, the show flew the pop flag high, with exuberant performances from Busted, Atomic Kitten, Blue and Ronan Keating. But, worryingly, August that year found weekly single sales at their lowest ebb since charts began! It was the following month, in an effort to combat the decline, that the first ever Download Chart was revealed – with Westlife at No.1.

Another real concern for long-time single-buying fans came that same year, when WH Smith announced that the chain would no longer be selling singles in its High Street stores. Though heaven only knows what the record buyers of 1964 would make of the 2004 No.1 by Eamon, entitled 'F**k It (I Don't Want You Back)'... Or indeed, Babyshambles, Marilyn Manson and Boogie Pimps – all of whom appeared on the *Pops* during the programme's 30th anniversary year. While Franz Ferdinand manfully flew the flag for indie rock.

In a last-ditch effort to compete against MTV, downloads, and *Pop Idol*, and for the first time ever, *Top of the Pops* on 30 July 2004 was broadcast completely live – from Gateshead's Baltic Square with performances from Girls Aloud, Busted, the ubiquitous Will Young and Jamelia.

However, by November the show's Friday night viewing figures had sunk below three million – mind you, it was up against the all–conquering *Coronation Street*. Still, the combination of low single sales and the corresponding lack of interest in the charts, led the BBC management to switch the show to Sunday evenings – and to BBC2. After 40 years on prime time, this was seen as proof-positive that *Top of the Pops* had run out of steam.

Music Week quoted BBC2 controller Roly Keating as being delighted to welcome *TOTP* to his channel. "It is an exciting new era for *TOTP*. We want to make it bigger and better, so that it becomes the ultimate pop music show for music lovers of every generation. BBC2 has a strong heritage in pop music and performance programmes, from *Later With Jools Holland* to Glastonbury, so *TOTP* will have a natural home on the channel."

BBC1 controller Lorraine Heggessey was also quoted: "*TOTP* has enjoyed a great life on BBC1, but I believe that moving to BBC2 and adapting to a more diverse audience of music lovers is the right evolution for the programme."

The Corporation's management insisted that *Top of the Pops* was being switched so that it would naturally follow on from Radio 1's official announcement of the new Top 40 chart. Which did make a certain amount of sense, as the immediacy of the new technology had made it seem positively antiquated to wait the best part of a week for a TV show to reflect a chart announced the previous Sunday.

Edition number 2,166 of *Top of the Pops* – the last to be shown on BBC1 (excepting Christmas and New Year specials) – was broadcast on 11 July 2005.

Six days later, at 7 pm on 17 July 2005, the show's first edition on BBC2 was broadcast, fronted by Fearne Cotton, who became one of the programme's longest-running regular presenters. After the move, Cotton continued to host with a different guest presenter each week, such as Rufus Hound or Richard Bacon. On a number of occasions however, occasional female guest presenters such as Lulu and Anastacia helped out.

But no matter what changes the powers-that-be at the Beeb made, it was never going to be enough... The final Friday night viewing figures had been nudging 2.5 million, the switch to Sunday saw them dip disastrously to 1.1 million. On one of those early Sunday evenings, *Pops* was trounced by *Antiques Roadshow*, *Emmerdale* and even *Carry On Up The Khyber*!

* * *

During 2005, both ends of the pop spectrum were in the ascendant; it proved to be the year of a former serving Army officer – James Blunt... But just when you thought you'd heard the last of mouthy Mancs, 'The Importance of Being Idle' gave Oasis their 8th No.1 single.

Controversy also returned to *TOTP* that year, when – introducing the Magic Numbers – Richard Bacon drew attention to the body weight of brother and sister act, describing them as "a fat melting pot of talent". Which, inevitably, caused a mighty rumpus, and a group walkout! And in the category of the tune you can't forget, even when you really, really try... came Crazy Frog and 'Axel F' providing irritation on an Olympic scale. The Frog even managed to stop Coldplay reaching No.1 with 'Speed Of Sound', despite Chris Martin's band playing a spirited *TOTP* performance in May 2005 – which concluded with him enthusing: "Thank you *Top of the Pops*. Thank you so much. You've been fantastic." Alison Goldfrapp also name-checked the show: in an interview, citing Goldfrapp's 'Ooh La La' as "harking back to Eno-era Roxy Music and old *Top of the Pops*."

One of 2005's most memorable singles was Kaiser Chiefs' 'I Predict A Riot'... While the chanteuses who popped in included the blissful Madeleine Peyroux; Charlotte Church in full rock-chick mode; and K.T. Tunstall at the beginning of her career. 'Electricity', from *Billy Elliot – The Musical*, gave Sir Elton John an incredible 63rd UK Top 40 hit. While at the other end of the scale, Barbados-born Rihanna made her chart debut with 'Pon De Replay'.

As ever, *Top of the Pops* reflected the year's chart; and that year's two biggest sellers were '(Is This the Way to) Amarillo?' (a revival of Tony Christie's 1971 original from Peter Kay and Comic Relief); and 'That's My Goal' (courtesy of *X Factor* winner, Shayne Ward).

It would prove to be the show's final year, but 2006 was a seismic year in the history of the UK pop charts. As expected, *X Factor* winner Leona Lewis triumphed, while Gnarls Barkley's 'Crazy' made history as the first single ever to top the charts on the basis of download sales alone! McFly and Keane also utilised the new technology, with singles available in totally new formats.

Looking back on the shows from that final year, one of the most poignant finds is Amy Winehouse, performing 'Rehab' on the show's Christmas edition. This was Amy before the fall. Amy resplendent: vamped up, with eyes as black as the Earl of Hell's waistcoat, and nails bloody as a gored matador. Amy in control and charismatic. And seeing her in action again reinforces what a loss she was.

It was early in 2006 that the triumph of that pesky new technology was finally confirmed, when the one *billionth* song was purchased from Apple's iTunes store. In spite of such success, figures at the time revealed that approximately 95% of all downloaded music in the UK was still illegal.

But in 2012, as CD sales continued to decline, and with HMV set to disappear from the High Street, iTunes went from strength to strength: drawing on its 26 million titles, 15,000 songs were being downloaded every *second* worldwide, and the ten billionth download took place in February 2013.

While the new technology boomed, more reflective souls remained troubled. Writing in the much-missed *Word* magazine, Paul Du Noyer spoke for many when he reflected: "Music… ought to be rationed, like bacon was during the war. If you had to queue all morning to get an hour of alt. country, or produce eight coupons for a minute of the Ramones, wouldn't you start loving it all more deeply again? We now live with a 24-hour, multi-platform delivery and the result is that we don't really listen to music any more. We just hear it."

Further evidence of the power of the internet and cyberspace came when Sandi Thom's debut single 'I Wish I Was A Punk Rocker (With Flowers In My Hair)' reached No.1 in June 2006. History claims her as the first chart-topper spawned by the internet – it was her performance of the song from a Tooting basement which spurred it on. Though it was surely more than coincidence that the single actually reached No.1 on the back of Sandi's *Top of the Pops* debut… And the song's chart success was due to its physical release by a major label –

which earned some criticism that Thom's success was merely an elaborate hype.

In the wake of Sandi Thom, came Lily Allen – hailed as the "Queen of MySpace", although she was actually signed to EMI at the time! But as MySpace was launching in the UK at the time, it didn't hurt having the vivacious Lily as its poster girl. At the other end of the telescope, folk favourite Kate Rusby also appeared on the programme toward the end of its life: "the Barnsley nightingale" was Ronan Keating's guest on his 'All Over Again' hit of 2006.

Further cyber success came courtesy of Arctic Monkeys; while not driven by social networking, it was hearing the band's music online that helped position them as the biggest UK breakthrough of 2006. As Peter Robinson wrote, looking back on the year in *The Word*: "The story here is really fairly pedestrian: people heard music, people liked music, people bought music. At the very least, however, the success of Arctic Monkeys put the web on a par with radio and television in terms of generating positive exposure."

The Sheffield band also joined the short but distinguished list of those who had boycotted *Top of the Pops*: following in the bolshie footsteps of Led Zeppelin and the Clash, Arctic Monkeys declined all invitations to appear live.

The axing of *Top of the Pops* came just months after another long-established landmark of the UK music scene disappeared; after 28 years the pop weekly *Smash Hits* had closed down. Writing in its review of 2006, *Music Week* commented: "Axing *Top of the Pops*… provoked outrage in the music industry… As the year draws to a close, the *TOTP* brand remains alive in the form of *TOTP2*… and with the traditional festive show scheduled for Christmas Day. Such a muddled vision for one of British TV's most valuable brands is perhaps to be expected given the Beeb's mismanagement of the show since the early Nineties."

As Kasabian's Sergio Pizzorno told Krissi Murison: "Music magazines aren't as big as they were, you can't get on television as a band and if you do it's 5am. There's no *Top of the Pops* where you can reach the masses. So the only real way of doing that and having that impact is Radio 1."

Art Brut revealed how they came close to making it onto the last *Top of the Pops*. The band, who had celebrated the UK chart show in their debut single 'Formed A Band', told nme.com that a fan petition almost got them included in the final edition. "Apparently there were about six and half thousand fans who signed a petition to try and get us on there," explained frontman Eddie Argos.

"Some kid started it and it just went from there. If we'd have had the chance we definitely would have done it and we'd have given it our best shot and had loads of fun. I reckon I'd have thrown some sort of breakdance in there."

Quoted in a *Q* feature, Mark Ratcliffe of "cultural trend analysts" Murmur confirmed: "People just won't sit down in front of a prime-time TV programme to watch eight songs they hate for every one song they love!"

But of course, it wasn't just music television which was under threat from the new order. In February 2006, Orson entered the record books when their 'No Tomorrow' reached No.1 in the UK; it remains the lowest-selling chart-topper in the 60 year history of the charts, with just 17,694 sales.

Still the show limped on, until the summer of 2006 when the plug was finally pulled. It was announced on 20 June 2006 that, after 42 years, the show was formally cancelled. The last-ever edition of *Top of the Pops* was broadcast on 30 July 2006, with Edith Bowman co-presenting its hour-long swansong, along with Jimmy Savile (who had also presented the first show), Reggie Yates, Mike Read, Pat Sharp, Sarah Cawood, Dave Lee Travis, Rufus Hound, Tony Blackburn and Janice Long... And, with its final breath, the show finally gave John Peel the opportunity to introduce Keith Harris & Orville.

The final day of recording on 26 July 2006 featured archive footage and tributes from guests including the Rolling Stones – the very first band to appear on *Top of the Pops*. Alongside the Stones were the Spice Girls, David Bowie, Wham!, Madonna, Beyoncé, Slade, Gnarls Barkley, Madonna, the Jackson 5, Sonny and Cher, and Robbie Williams. That last show wrapped up with a final countdown, topped by Shakira, as her track "Hips Don't Lie" (featuring Wyclef Jean) had climbed back up to No.1 on the UK Singles Chart earlier that day. And the show ended for ever with Savile turning the lights off in the empty studio.

Fearne Cotton, the regular presenter at the time, was unavailable to co-host for the final edition due to filming for ITV's *Love Island* in Fiji – but she did kick off the show with a quick introduction, recorded on location, saying "It's still number one, it's *Top of the Pops*." But since that final episode featured no acts live in the studio, the honour of being the last act ever to perform on a weekly episode of *TOTP* goes to Snow Patrol – the last act in the penultimate edition – with 'Chasing Cars'. BARB, the TV ratings organisation, reported the final show's viewing figures as 3.98 million.

Reflecting in 2009, John Niven (author of *Kill Your Friends*, one of the very best rock & roll novels) wrote: "Woolworth's. *Top of the Pops*. Demand. How impossibly nostalgic those words look now."

It was also in 2009 that a movement was started to try and break the stranglehold of *The X Factor* winner automatically becoming the Christmas No.1 ("as predictable as elections in North Korea" said *the Guardian*). DJ Jon Morter began a Facebook campaign to deny Joe McElderry's 'The Climb' the Xmas No.1 spot – and amazingly he succeeded, with the profane Rage Against the Machine's 'Killing in the Name' doing the business.

Even three years after the demise of the weekly show, *Top of the Pops* was still very much part of the BBC's festive programming: the 2009 *TOTP* New Year's special (featuring the hapless Joe McElderry, Alexandra Burke, Florence + the Machine and Robbie Williams) pulled in nearly five million viewers. The brand was clearly still alive and kicking – and the success of the festive special prompted renewed requests for the programme to be reinstated in the weekly schedules. A new Facebook campaign, instigated once again by Jon Morter, had within hours attracted 3,000 supporters. And in 2011, BBC4 began regularly re-running vintage *Top of the Pops* shows from the 1970s, attracting respectable viewing figures.

Looking back in October 2012, following the news that Channel 4 were canning their music show *T4*, *Music Week* editor Tim Ingham wrote: "By the end, the BBC's wheezing resignation and plasticine pride had probably become as recognizable to the music industry as *Top of the Pops* itself. That's wheezing after years of being given the runaround by on-demand copyright prankster YouTube; plasticine after having to bend and remold those 'fond farewell' and 'committed passion for music' platitudes anew for each and every *TOTP* demotion.

"When the show which helped so many of us bound through adolescence hit the skids by July 2006 after 42 years, it was looking bruised, frail and freakishly fizzed-up. It had recently been shunted from BBC1 to BBC2, from Fridays to Sundays and – most harmfully – from a seven million audience to a one million audience in less than a decade. The Beeb now exhausted of quick fixes, concluded that you simply couldn't make a popular music-based TV entertainment show work on these channels at these times."

The growth of new technology had certainly helped kill off the show. *Q* magazine pointed out that in the year leading up to the final *Top of the Pops*, 'A Million Ways' by the Chicago group OK Go had become the most downloaded music video ever. Its nine million YouTube views contrasting sharply with the one million who were watching *Top of the Pops* towards the end of its run – emphasising just how far the music industry had come from that disused church in Manchester in a previous century.

Soon after that last show, Ian Gittins wrote: "Who killed *TOTP*? An uncaring media world watched it perish. Andi Peters' fingerprints were arguably on the smoking gun – but in truth, it died of old age..." He also quoted one of the original presenters, Pete Murray, who said: "Let's face it, it ran for nearly as long as *The Mousetrap*. Maybe that's what *TOTP* was – *The Mousetrap* of music TV!"

It may be a cliché, but the end of *Top of the Pops* really did mark the end of an era. The high watermark of the programme came at a time when popular music from the British Isles genuinely did rule the world's airwaves. The Beatles and Rolling Stones; Pink Floyd and David Bowie; these were artists who reached out across the globe, affecting music, fashion, sexual mores, even society itself. And for many of those pioneers, their first step on that global rung began with that crucial, eagerly-anticipated debut on *Top of the Pops*.

Writing this book has brought back a lifetime (that's like... almost a gigabyte) of memories... of the changing fashions and unforgettable music, of those gone before and those still persevering. And so many of those memories are linked to that weekly television programme which gave you not just the sound, but the sight, of that timeless music. And what sounds they were – 'A Whiter Shade Of Pale', 'Jean Genie', 'Merry Xmas Everybody', 'Pretty Vacant', 'Don't Look Back In Anger', 'Elephant Stone'...

But as so many people have testified, the programme was always bigger than any of the bands who appeared on it; bigger than any of the presenters, dancers or producers. And it lives on, not just in memory, but in compilations, and repeats scattered across the night-time networks for nostalgic insomniacs.

Stumbling across these glimpses of the past can be a mildly disconcerting experience though. You can forgive the fashions and hairstyles, the cravats and the Zapata moustaches... but watching those old shows *now*, you already know the future. You can see the disintegration, despair and death that awaits so many of those eager-to-please young acts. Back then it seemed like there was no tomorrow – Graham Nash, happy to be a Hollie; the Dave Clark 5 convinced their Tottenham-sound would soon eclipse the Beatles; Brian Jones, cool and confident, when the Rolling Stones were still *his* band...

There they all are, grinning and buoyant in their Dougie Millings' suits, teeth gleaming from all that free school milk. Barely out of their teens, barely able to believe their luck… The war children, moulded by the NHS, the 11+ and skiffle. Now they look more like the title of another long-running television programme of the period, *All Our Yesterdays*.

* * *

In hindsight, probably the defining *Top of the Pops* moment was David Bowie and 'Starman', the song that gave birth to Ziggy Stardust, launched the 1970s, and remains a primal moment of popular culture television. Apt then, that as I write, the world is convulsing to 'Where Are We Now', a new single by an act who's been out of the limelight for a decade… the man who *told* the world, David Bowie.

But the simple truth is that the landscape which made possible a programme like *Top of the Pops* back in 1964, has changed so completely that it is inconceivable to imagine it ever returning. With today's immediate access to news and music, who would be willing to wait seven whole days to see and hear their favourite music?

However, nothing that has come since – no matter how exciting – can diminish the impact that this programme had during its heyday. The BBC's Stanley Appel, who had a long association with the programme over the years, summed it up nicely: "*Top of the Pops* – it was like switching on the gas! It was just *there*, every Thursday night at 7.30!"

Writing in 2012 Mark Cooper reflected: "As Head of Music Entertainment at the BBC, I often get asked about that great British music institution, *Top of the Pops*. Will we bring back the weekly series? Why did we pull it? People get really nostalgic about the programme – me included, I love it. But the circumstances that created *Top of the Pops* have changed forever. People who don't think that are being sentimental. We've all grown up and we've all changed. You'd love *Top of the Pops* to exist, and so would I, but would you tune in every week? When 18 million people watched it in the 70s it was the only game in town and television was everything. But it's such a different world now."

Just imagine telling a Beatle fan in 1965 that any period of the Fabs' eight year recorded history could be accessed at the press of a button on your telephone. Or a Smiths admirer that every facet of Morrissey's career was available in under a second on your home computer. What sort of Rihanna fan would wait for longer than the blink of an eye for news of their idol's every move, in public and private? It is all that, and so much more, that contributed to the inevitable decline, not only of *Top of the Pops*, but also the entire UK record industry.

The tumbling sales of CDs continues, leading to speculation that the end of physical ownership of albums may now be in sight. At the time of writing, the demise of HMV has been announced, although there is some hope is that it may survive in a demonstrably stripped-down form. But after 90 years, its removal from the High Street is just another nail in the coffin of the music we grew up with.

And, talking of the music we grew up with... can it really be the case that music by those pioneering legends Elvis Presley, Cliff Richard, Bob Dylan and the Beatles is now in the public domain? That effectively, and officially, means that the music we grew up with is now history.

Top of the Pops too must now be firmly consigned to the museum of memory. Despite the odd DVD release or archive repeat, its only true home is as a wallow in the warm jacuzzi of nostalgia. But what memories they are... You only need to hear that *TOTP* theme and you are transported back to spotty, uncertain adolescence... the trepidation of O-Level results... the first steps toward your chosen career... those first faltering kisses and glorious fashion catastrophes... uncertain hairstyles... rollicking rides on a musical rollercoaster...

And if you are now older than the programme itself, you too will soon be crossing the Rubicon – perhaps with the realization that you have become your parents, as you rail to anyone who will listen "What is this rubbish?" "It hasn't got a tune!" "Is that a boy or a girl?"

In June 2103, the chocolate maker Cadbury's conducted a survey to find the top things we would like to see make a comeback... and there in its rightful place at No.1 – way ahead of *Baywatch*, Gordon the Gopher, and ghetto blasters – was *Top of the Pops* with 41% of the vote.

But, like it or not, the show is gone for good. It will never return in the weekly format we grew up with, and no replacement could ever match the impact of the programme we watched diligently every Thursday night. Few television programmes ever have enjoyed such resonance. Which is why it was No.1; why it was, and always will be, *Top of the Pops*!

CHAPTER 6 Music and Fashion 1964–2006 by Eddi Fiegel

From Land's End to Lanarkshire, from Dover to Dumfries, between 1964 and 2006, teenagers across Britain not only got a weekly burst of music from *Top of the Pops* but also rare glimpses of fashions they would otherwise often never have seen.

Top of the Pops opened a window onto the newest, hippest and sometimes most daring fashions sported by pop stars and musicians, and in turn brought inspiration to thousands, particularly those living beyond the cities, in suburbs or rural areas.

Whether it was the Beatles in their collarless suits; David Bowie with his Starman feathered haircut; Madonna in fingerless black lace gloves or 90s rappers kitted out in sportswear and head-to-toe bling, these stars' appearances often unwittingly spawned nationwide trends. But equally importantly, they also brought hope to those who viewed themselves as misfits or different in any way, providing them with welcome glimpses of how one could express oneself, take a non-conformist stance and go against the grain, at least in one's dress sense, if nothing else.

* * *

When the Beatles appeared on *Top of the Pops* with 'Can't Buy Me Love' in March 1964, viewers not only got a chance to see their floppy fringed mop-tops in head-shaking action but also their collarless suits and Cuban-heeled boots.

At the suggestion of manager Brian Epstein, the Liverpudlian combo had visited Soho tailor Dougie Millings. They had a specific request. "Make us something different" they had told him. "Don't make us look like the Shadows!" The result was the Pierre Cardin-inspired suits which the four championed alongside Italian-style boots from London theatrical shoe-makers Anello and

LEFT: As well as shattering musical barriers, punk trashed the fashion industry

Davide. It was a look which would soon be considered 'groovy' and 'gear' by teenagers in droves.

The Beatles' first single 'Love Me Do' in 1962 had coincided with the emergence of the Carnaby Street 'Mod' and 'Swinging London' styles which would come to epitomise the first half of the decade. Starting in London and the Southeast, the vogue in male dress for slick, tailor-made Italian-influenced suits with narrow lapels, button-down collar shirts and thin ties had grown out of the jazz and beatnik movements and was indicative of the newly affluent post-war teenage generation. The Who and Small Faces epitomised the scene's ethos of being cool, sharply dressed and neat with fastidious attention to detail such as a jacket's lining, pocket stitching or collar.

The female Mod look was similarly pioneered by pop stars such as Cilla Black, another Liverpudlian from Brian Epstein's roster. Black was seen sporting a Vidal Sassoon short bobbed haircut with the release of her 1964 No. 1 'Anyone Who Had A Heart' accompanied by the type of Mary Quant mini dress which was revolutionising British fashion. Instead of hem lines being dictated by Parisian couture houses and the style arbiters of *Vogue* magazine, the young Quant had inaugurated thigh-skimming, A-line minis and bold, geometric prints. Similarly Sandie Shaw introduced young girls to glamorous, yet unquestionably young, fashions which seemed to shout 'freedom' from the rooftops and thumb their nose at the staid styles of their mothers' generation.

As the decade moved on, the Carnaby Street 'Swinging London' Mod look gave way to looser, floating styles that came with the discovery by London's pop elite of psychedelic drugs. A fascination with all things vintage, in particular Victoriana (and miltaria for men) became all the rage. The new dandyish modes inspired by the cravat and floppy hat wearing Aesthetes of the 19th century, like Aubrey Beardsley and Oscar Wilde, were soon seen on everyone from the Rolling Stones, Procol Harum and Jimi Hendrix to the Beatles, notably in their promotional films for the double A-sided single 'Strawberry Fields Forever'/'Penny Lane' in 1967.

Similarly, by the late 60s and early 70s, the Victorian and Edwardian influence was also being championed for women by Laura Ashley with her high-necked, tight-waisted midi and maxi dresses, as seen on *Top of the Pops* worn by dance troupe Pan's People.

Around this time, the romantic look also began to give way to ideas influenced

David Bowie, with his Starman feathered haircut, in quintessential Ziggy mode, TOTP, 1972

by the 1930s, particularly in the styles of two of the most influential designers of the day: Biba (the brand name of designer Barbara Hulanicki) and Ossie Clark. Biba's Kensington store soon became the de rigueur hang-out for pop stars, beautiful people and aspiring hipsters alike, championing a world of velvet suits, feather boas, floppy hats, glamorous flapper dresses and beaded skull caps. Ossie Clark meanwhile – whose creations were seen on stars including the Beatles, Rolling Stones and Marianne Faithfull – reincarnated the long, figure-hugging bias-cut dresses of the 30s as well as devising a more rock & roll look of snakeskin jackets and hot pants.

It was not a huge leap from these styles to what was gradually to become the look inextricably tied in with the "we love to boogie" re-imagined rock & roll that was Glam rock. It was a style that was to have a huge impact on virtually everyone who saw it. When ex-Mod Marc Bolan appeared on *Top of the Pops* in 1971 with 'Hot Love' he had glitter sprinkled on his face and wore a silvery white satin jacket and trousers. In July of the following year, when another ex-Mod – David Bowie, made his now legendary appearance with 'Starman' – it was not only the all round other-worldliness of the song and its lyrics, and its compellingly catchy melody that entranced audiences, but also Bowie's androgynous multi-coloured jumpsuit, heavily made up face and choppy, feathered haircut. This last feature in particular was to prove hugely influential and sent teenagers across Britain, including a young George O'Dowd (later Boy George) dashing off to their local barbers with (often unsuccessful) requests to try and replicate the cut.

Glam rock was soon the rage with everyone from art bands like Roxy Music (both singer Bryan Ferry with his effete lounge-lizard look in slick, Antony Price suits, and keyboardist Brian Eno with his feather boas, face paint and skin-tight satin loons) to the more mainstream likes of the Sweet, and pop groups Abba and Boney M championing the look.

✳ ✳ ✳

By the middle of the '70s, the last vestiges of 60s optimism were long gone. With unemployment growing and utility strikes a regular occurrence, fashion had become similarly downbeat. Glam rock had been overtaken by pub and progressive rock, both of which very much played down any attempt at stylistic glamour. The time was therefore ready for a new sound and indeed a new look, which duly arrived in the form of punk.

Sex Pistols manager Malcolm McLaren and his fashion designer partner Vivienne Westwood had between them devised a newly trashy, deeply provocative and anti-establishment look, comprising bondage trousers and ripped, anti-Royalist T-shirts as devised by the Situationist-inspired artist Jamie Reid. It was a look which was to have one of the most profound and far-reaching influences on fashion of any musical movement.

But while bondage trousers, tartan, safety-pins and wackily-coloured Mohican haircuts would become the clichéd styles associated with punk in years to come, the punk aesthetic was in fact much more significantly individualistic. In keeping with the original do-it-yourself, anti-fashion punk ethos, genuine punks were just as likely to wear deeply unfashionable clothes found in charity shops as those created by the young designers in the burgeoning nationwide market stalls and independent shops sprouting up as part of the movement.

Punk was not however to everyone's taste; even for those who were still young. Others were often more interested in the wide-lapelled suits and floaty knee-length dresses associated with the then newly emerging sounds of disco as presented by the likes of American acts Chic, Sister Sledge and Diana Ross and subsequently Britain's own Bee Gees with their chart-topping soundtrack to *Saturday Night Fever*.

Punk was nevertheless to have the longest legacy. At the end of the 70s, viewers were introduced to Coventry bands like the Specials and the Selecter who had formed the 2-Tone movement. With its message of racial harmony and social commentary on life in the inner cities of recession-dominated Britain, 2-Tone also carried a strong visual look of its own. Youths around Britain were soon seen sporting the pork pie hats, tonic suits, Sta-prest trousers, black and white lapel badges and eyeliner – as seen on *Top of the Pops* by the likes of the Specials' Terry Hall, whilst young girls similarly donned the masculine bomber jackets and badges championed by the Selecter's Pauline Black.

Musically, the 2-Tone bands had been inspired by the ska and reggae sounds of yesteryear which they had heard in the Caribbean immigrant communities around them whilst growing up, and in the same way, bands like the Jam, Merton Parkas, Secret Affair and the Lambrettas – all of whom appeared on *Top of the Pops* around this time, looked back to the Mod groups of the 60s for inspiration.

These bands sparked a nationwide mini-Mod revival and in its wake, thousands of young boys rushed out to copy Paul Weller's Steve Marriott-

The Long Wait: a 1960s Top of the Pops *audience at a camera rehearsal*

inspired haircut and recreate his Mod-inspired suits whilst young girls donned the Swinging London monochrome minis of the earlier decade. The revival however proved short-lived and as the recession wore on into the early 80s, another London-based movement was to take a similarly retro reaction to the economic climate, albeit in a rather different way.

* * *

Like the 'Bright Young Things' of the 1920s and 30s, the groups subsequently monikered 'The New Romantics' embraced colourful escapism and hedonism, and synthesiser dominated groups like Spandau Ballet and Visage were soon seen on *Top of the Pops* garbed in outlandish combinations of 1940s demob-style peg trousers and wedge haircuts, crisp white shirts and Bonnie Prince Charlie-ish tartan shawls pinned over their shoulders.

The look was never to become as widespread beyond Britain's cities, but hot on its heels, another scene – this time the post-punk indie movement, was to have a far broader stylistic influence. In November 1983 the Smiths made their *Top of the Pops* debut performing 'This Charming Man' with Morrissey brandishing the now famous gladioli.

Morrissey's 50s-influenced quiff and subsequent appearances in standard issue National Health glasses were to influence a generation of students and indie-music fans. Equally de rigueur for both men and women, the look comprised short, heavily gelled, spiked haircuts, black suede pointed boots and outsized men's overcoats as seen on similarly guitar-based 'indie' bands like Echo & the Bunnymen. These were invariably bought from a vintage emporium at one of the by-now ubiquitous nationwide markets and second-hand stalls which had continued to flourish since the emergence of punk.

Indie girls meanwhile frequented the same sources, stocking up on 50s floral print dresses, accompanied by flat pumps – and occasionally Minnie Mouse style headscarves tied around their choppy haircuts, as seen on popstars from indie star Tracey Thorn of Everything But The Girl to more mainstream, but hip acts like Altered Images' Clare Grogan and even the chart-topping Bananarama.

The 80s was a decade of tribalism in youth fashions and one in which a style of dress instantly identified you as a follower of a certain type of music. This was unquestionably true of the 'indie' look and at least as much so with one of the other major trends of the decade – Goth. Inextricably linked to post-punk bands like Siouxsie & Banshees, the Sisters of Mercy and the Cure – all of whom favoured dyed-black, heavily back-combed, spiky hair, dramatic make-up (for men and women alike) usually featuring heavy black eyeliner and liberal dousings of violet blusher, black and purple lace (for women) and black drainpipe trousers for men – it was to be a style which would continue to resonate with future generations in the years to come.

But not all influences were home-grown. Madonna's 1984 appearances on *Top of the Pops*, with 'Holiday' and 'Like A Virgin' also spawned thousands of female imitators countrywide, eager to copy her Boy George-style, rag-tailed blonde hairdo and pseudo-Goth, charity-shop chic look, complete with punkish studded wristbands, Aerobics-style leg-warmers and black fingerless lace gloves. But it was to be two other American imports – House music and Hip Hop, which would have the most significant impact, both musically and visually on subsequent decades.

* * *

At the end of the 80s, the sounds of House and Hip Hop which were emerging in New York and Chicago began to filter across the Atlantic. Initially they were admired by musical cognoscenti in Britain's cities but soon a homegrown reaction began to evolve in the form of Britain's own Acid House.

First heard in cities like London and Manchester, acts like A Guy Called Gerald, D-Mob and S'Express all had hits in 1988 with 'Voodoo Ray', 'We Call it Acieed' and 'Theme From S'Express' respectively. What they all had in common visually was a decidedly dressed-down, anti-glam approach to fashion, favouring instead the tracksuit tops and bottoms, trainers and general sportswear look championed by American House and Hip Hop acts.

In Manchester, the style briefly morphed into the 'baggy' look initially associated with local bands like the Happy Mondays and Stone Roses who took the sportswear notion a step further with particularly loose-fitting, 'baggy' shirts and trousers of their own. At the same time, two other indie movements were emerging which similarly downplayed any attempt at stylistic flourishes. In Britain, guitar-based acts such as My Bloody Valentine, Slowdive and Ride were garnering the nickname 'shoe-gazers' for their preference for decidedly untheatrical performances, generally dressed-down appearance and overall fondness for staring at their shoes rather than their audience.

From America meanwhile, the influential and similarly guitar-heavy but harder, punkier 'grunge' scene was throwing up bands like Nirvana who appeared on *Top of the Pops* in 1991 with 'Smells Like Teen Spirit'. Even beyond dressing-down, grunge seemed to positively encourage an all-round unkempt ethos which soon became virtually a look in itself to its legions of followers, not just in Britain but worldwide.

But in tandem with grunge, over the next few years, it was the new wave of British guitar-based pop bands who would come to define one of the most far-reaching styles with Britpop. Whilst still resolutely championing a self-consciously nonchalant predilection for loose, dressed-down sportswear, bands like Blur, Oasis, Suede and Elastica would formalise the look slightly with their incorporation of retro elements such as 60s-style airline flight bags, bowling bags and, in the case of Blur's Damon Albarn and Oasis's Liam Gallagher, Mod-inspired haircuts.

*** * ***

Britpop however was to be relatively shortlived and by the end of the 90s and dawn of the next decade, it was to be the American dance, Hip Hop and R'n'B scenes which would continue to dominate fashions. Acts like the Fugees and rappers such as Puff Daddy (aka Sean Coombs), with their fondness for large amounts of showy gold jewellery, diamanté – or 'bling' as it would come to be known, had widespread influence over teenagers across the UK in a look which continues to prevail two decades on. Later, towards the end of *Top of the Pops'* run, rapper Pharrell Williams, would become widely viewed as a fashion icon himself, launching both men and women's fashion lines in 2005.

In 2013 the crossover between music and fashion is the stuff of big business and no longer the preserve of audacious new young designers. Global stars such as Stella McCartney and fashion houses such as Gucci regularly collaborate with major names in rock and pop, whilst pop stars such as Madonna and even ex-pop stars like Victoria Beckham have become fashion designers themselves. But the relationship no longer carries the potency, influence or fervently youth-oriented charge of *Top of the Pops'* heyday in the 60s, 70s and 80s, when both music and fashion conveyed something significant about who you were, and not just the clothes you wore.

Harry Goodwin:
Uncrowned King of Pop Photography

It was while he was serving in the RAF during World War II that Harry Goodwin started taking photos. What began as a hobby stood Harry in good stead when the BBC launched the legendary *Top of the Pops* in 1964. Producer Johnnie Stewart needed a safe pair of hands to photograph the acts as they performed in the studio at Dickenson Road, and as he was already based in Manchester, had seen his work printed in the local papers *and* was working as a scene shifter on the BBC's *Good Old Days*, Harry was the producer's first call. Between 1964 and 1973, Harry was there for the glory years as the official photographer for *Top of the Pops*.

Manchester-born Harry was set to follow in his father's footsteps as a bookmaker, but wartime service, and the increasing awareness of just how lucrative photographing celebrities could be, saw Harry persevere behind the lens. After the war Harry returned to Manchester where he became a freelance photographer, with his first commission being shots of the Scotland footballer Ephraim 'Jock' Dodds. Harry was also a familiar figure in Manchester's sporting world – he became friends with Sir Alex Ferguson whom he had met whilst he was managing Aberdeen. He told Andy Peden Smith that, 'A highlight of my life was being invited to Old Trafford to meet Sir Alex and see some of my photos displayed in the canteen there.' During the 1950s though Harry mainly worked at beauty pageants and on the boxing circuit – one of his heroes was Muhammad Ali.

By the end of 1963 however he was approached about a new series called *Top of the Pops* which was scheduled to last 6 weeks. Little did Harry know that this 6 week stint was to last until the end of 1973! Harry was disappointed at the £30 a week the BBC originally offered, but was guaranteed six photos used every week, and a screen credit at the programme's end. His abiding memory of that first programme was a fist fight with the Rolling Stones' Brian Jones who was not happy being snapped. He also has a vivid memory of nearly coming to blows with Dusty Springfield, but also recalls Cher sending a limo to collect him.

Left: Harry Goodwin portrait of Shirley Bassey in January 1968, caught between James Bond themes

During his 9 years on the show, Harry was always there – in Manchester or London, at rehearsal and in performance – to snap the pop firmament's brightest stars. Harry's photos offer a revealing insight of rock legends Jimi Hendrix, the Who, Jackson 5, Sonny & Cher, Stevie Wonder, Dusty Springfield, the Rolling Stones, Rod Stewart, John Lennon, Elton John, Marc Bolan, the Supremes and his own personal favourites, the Bee Gees and Sandie Shaw. In fact, over the years, Harry reckons there are only two chart acts he *never* photographed: Frank Sinatra and Elvis Presley. Harry's position gave him the opportunity to build a unique record of almost every pop star to appear on the programme – probably more than any other rock photographer. Bee Gee Barry Gibb said, 'He's a legend. I don't think there's any artist who hasn't been photographed by this man.'

Status Quo in 1968, during an early Top of the Pops *appearance - they went on to become the* group *who made most appearances. (Note* TOTP *photographer Harry Goodwin hard at work in front)*

The Beatles prior to their first and only Top of the Pops *appearance, 1966*

Stanley Dorfman, the programme's co-producer and editor, said "I'm as proud to have worked with him as I am to have worked with any of the great rock and roll stars because I think he's part of that whole Sixties scene…".

Harry got on with most of the stars on the programme making friends with many of them. This wasn't the case all the time though as he discovered when first photographing the Beatles. 'John Lennon could be a right one' he remembered. However, when Lennon went solo he invited Harry to take some shots and '…he introduced me to Yoko as the greatest photographer in Britain. It shocked me but then I realised I didn't make him feel uncomfortable.'

As well as the *Top of the Pops* studio, Harry also snapped the acts who were performing in Manchester, and his photos of the Beatles and Bob Dylan are timeless.

Harry has some great memories of acts who appeared on the show over the years, and glad he took Mick Jagger's advice to stick out for more than the £30 a week the BBC originally offered. And even though he never achieved his ambition

to be more famous than Mick Jagger, Harry Goodwin did okay for himself!

Harry's photographic legacy remains. There is a series of photos at John Lennon Airport in Liverpool because of his relationship with John Lennon and eleven of his portraits, including images of Sandie Shaw and individual photographs of each of the Beatles, are now part of the National Portrait Gallery collection. The BBC erased many of the early *TOTP* programmes so in many cases it is only Goodwin's black and white iconic images that remain as a record of their performances.

The Bee Gees (Robin, Barry and Maurice Gibb) shot in 1967, at the time of their first Top of the Pops *appearance*

Those *Top of the Pops* Themes in Full...

1964–1973 'Percussion Piece' (played by Bobby Midgley and the *TOTP* Orchestra)

1973–1981 'Whole Lotta Love' (performed by CCS, written, ironically by Led Zeppelin, who always refused to appear on the programme)

1981–1986 'Yellow Pearl' (Phil Lynott)

1986–1991 'The Wizard' (Paul Hardcastle)

1991–1995 'Now Get Out Of That' (Tony Gibber)

1995–1997 'Red Hit Pop' (Vince Clarke)

1998–2003 'Whole Lotta Love' (Drums 'n' bass version by Ben Chapman)

2003–2006 'Now Get Out Of That' (Remixed by Tony Gibber)

Across

8   She topped the charts with her Young debut single in 2012 (6)

9   Genre that includes Tinie Tempah's chart-topping Pass Out (3)

10 He claimed to be Lonely in 2005 but enough fans bought his single to keep it at the top two weeks running (4)

11 Like Eminem's kind of soldiers (3)

12 Mambo king whose Cherry Pink And Apple Blossom White also provided a No.1 for Eddie Calvert's cover version (5, 5)

14 Fame-maker Irene located amid The Housemartins' Caravan Of Love (4)

15 ---- -- Breaking My Heart, Elton's first chart-topper, achieved in partnership with Kiki Dee (3'1, 2)

18 She chewed up males according to this Hall and Oates US No.1 (8)

19 Spanish DJ whose Loca People was a chart-topper across Europe (3, 4)

20 How The Hollies confirmed that they were still breathing in 1965 (1'1, 5)

24 His Dizzy hit returned to the top when Vic Reeves met The Wonder Stuff (5, 3)

27 They sound broke but their No.1s included Who's David?, Thunderbirds and Crashed The Wedding (6)

29 I Got You --- Sonny & Cher's debut hit later revived by UB40 with Chrissie Hynde (4)

30 Label that first released Kylie Minogue's Spinning Around (10)

33 This Guy's In Love With You lyricist David (3)

34 His song Grace Kelly also mentioned Freddie Mercury (4)

35 The Sun Always Shines On TV they declared in 1985 (1-2)

36 Piper who notched three chart-toppers in the late '90s (6)

Down

1   It's certain that this Take That song was composed jointly by Gary Barlow, Robbie Williams and Mark Owen. (4)

2   This upwardly mobile Gabrielle hit sampled Dylan's Knockin' On Heaven's Door (4)

3   Maroon 5 telephonic hit that featured Wiz Khalifa (8)

4   Another Level took this up to the top (5, 2)

5   Where Billy Joel and Westlife's girl came from (6)

6   I Can't Stop Loving You he declared during 1962 (3, 7)

7   How Adam Faith felt sorry for himself in 1960 (4, 2)

13 Band On The --- proved a US No.1 for Paul McCartney & Wings in 1974 (3)

16 Rita whose R.I.P. was originally penned for Rihanna (3)

17 Drummer whom, with guitarist Jet Harris, struck gold with Diamonds (4, 6)

21 This vocalist was pink with yellow spots (2, 6)

22 Bobby who implored Take Good Care Of My Baby, a US No.1 in 1961 (3)

23 With whom Myleene Klass and Kym Marsh delivered a Pure And Simple success (4,3)

25 Cinderella Rockefella's Esther and Abi (6)

26 One more time for this No.1 by Iyaz (6)

28 Frankie Goes To Hollywood's number of tribes (3)

31 Did The Beatles really need such assistance in 1965? (4)

32 Ain't No Doubt that this was a hit for Jimmy from Auf Wiedersehen Pet (4)

The *Top of the Pops* Crossword

57 Things You Never Knew About *Top of the Pops*...

1. The programme has been mentioned in songs by the Rezillos, Boomtown Rats, the Kinks and Mott the Hoople.

2. It was originally commissioned for six weeks – it ran for 42 years!

3. The very first edition was broadcast at 6.35pm on BBC Television, 1 January 1964.

4. Despite having the No.1 single ('I Want To Hold Your Hand'); the No.3 single ('She Loves You'); two EPs (*The Beatles Hits; Twist & Shout*) and their second *LP* (*With The Beatles*) in the Top 20 – the Beatles did *not* appear on that historic first programme.

5. The first *Top of the Pops* had the following acts miming live in the studio: Dusty Springfield ('I Only Want To Be With You'); the Rolling Stones ('I Wanna Be Your Man'); the Dave Clark Five ('Glad All Over'); the Hollies ('Stay') and the Swinging Blue Jeans ('Hippy Hippy Shake'). On film, Cliff Richard and the Shadows performed 'Don't Talk To Him'; Freddie & the Dreamers ('You Were Made For Me'). The studio audience were shown dancing to the Beatles 'She Loves You' and Gene Pitney's '24 Hours From Tulsa'.

6. The first shows were broadcast from a former church on Dickenson Road, Manchester.

7. The air fare from London to Manchester then was £9/14/- (£9.70p).

8. For their appearance on 29 April 1964, the Rolling Stones received £86.00.

9. Original producer Johnnie Stewart (1917-2005) called it "the simplest show in the world – and pure murder to put on!"

10. The programme moved to London, and the first show broadcast from the capital was on 20 January 1966, and featured Cilla Black, Otis Redding, Paul & Barry Ryan, David & Jonathan, Crispian St Peters, Herman's Hermits, Stevie Wonder, Herb Alpert and the Spencer Davis Group.

11. The only time the Beatles did appear live (to mime!) on the show was 16 June 1966 when the Fab Four reported to BBC TV Centre to plug both sides of their current single, 'Paperback Writer' and 'Rain'.

12. Sir Cliff Richard has appeared on *Top of the Pops* more than any other performer, with an estimated 160 appearances.

13. The last time Pink Floyd appeared on the show was in July 1967, the Floyd's Syd Barrett reasoned that if John Lennon didn't have to appear, then neither did he.

14. Lulu met her future husband, Maurice Gibb, on the show in 1967 when the Bee Gees were making their UK television debut.

15. Pete Townshend admitted it was *TOTP* which prompted him into his famous windmill style of playing the guitar: "Keith Moon would get about 80% of the camera time, so every time it came to me, I would swing my arm like a maniac".

16. Dance troupe Pan's People made their *TOTP* debut in 1968, dancing to Tommy James & the Shondells' 'Mony Mony'.

17. John Peel grudgingly made his *TOTP* debut the same year, then forgot the name of the act he was supposed to introduce – he wasn't asked back until 1982!

18. Status Quo are the group with more *TOTP* appearances (1968-2006) than any other – 86 in total.

19. Prior to his landmark 1972 'Starman' appearance, David Bowie had been on *TOTP* in 1969 performing 'Space Oddity' and in 1971 playing piano behind Peter Noone who had a hit with Bowie's 'Oh You Pretty Thing'.

20. Elton John's first *TOTP* appearances were as a backing musician behind Brotherhood of Man and Pickettywitch in 1970.

21. At its high point during the early 1970s, it was estimated that 25% of the UK television audience was watching *TOTP* on a Thursday evening.

22. Ironically, the *Top of the Pops* theme 1973-1981 was Led Zeppelin's 'Whole Lotta Love' (performed by CCS). Ironic because Zeppelin never released a single in the UK while they were active, and thus never appeared on the show.

23. Between January and September 1971 the show featured an album slot – Yes, Fairport Convention and Caravan were only some of the acts who appeared.

24. It was in April 1971 when T.Rex appeared on the programme – Marc Bolan threw some glitter on his cheeks, and thus Glam Rock was born!

25. Looking for his outrageous costume to wear on *Top of the Pops*, Slade's Dave Hill would scour Kensington Market, where he was served by one Freddie Mercury!

26. When Queen made their *TOTP* debut, Freddie didn't even own a television set, so had to watch himself in a shop window on Oxford Street.

27. The most influential *TOTP* appearance ever? That would be July 1972, when David Bowie appeared as Ziggy Stardust promoting 'Starman' – Marc Almond, Gary Kemp, Holly Johnson, Ian McCulloch and Gary Numan all remember that one performance.

28. Bowie performing 'Jean Genie' on *TOTP* on 4 January 1973 was thought lost forever, until in 2012 when a BBC cameraman revealed he'd kept a copy.

29. The biggest act on *TOTP* during 1975? Their name would be... Mud! 45 weeks on the charts during the year...

30. Pan's People quit *TOTP* in April 1976 (dancing to the Four Seasons 'Silver Star') and were replaced by...

31. Ruby Flipper only lasted six months, before being replaced by Legs & Co.

32. Julie Covington ('Don't Cry For Me Argentina') never appeared promoting the song from *Evita*, but is one of an elite group (Leona Lewis, Alexandra Burke and Adele): only four British female singers have sold a million copies of a single in the UK.

33. DJ "Diddy" David Hamilton remembers being surprised at how little he got paid for presenting the programme in 1976 – £100.

34. The Jam were the first punk group to appear on *TOTP*, in April 1977, promoting their first single, 'In The City'.

35. Famously the Clash boycotted the show because they'd have to mime – ironically, on the back of a TV jeans ad, their 1982 song 'Should I Stay Or Should I Go' was a UK No.1.

36. Clash frontman Joe Strummer finally appeared on *TOTP* in 1996, alongside Lily Allen's dad Keith in Black Grape on the Euro '96 anthem 'England's Irie'.

37. In December 1977, Elton John made *TOTP* history when he became the first non-DJ to present the programme.

38. Memorable *TOTP* encounters – the Wurzels and Bob Marley; the Buzzcocks and Brotherhood Of Man; Slade and the Osmonds; the Wedding Present and Jason Donovan...

39. In 1981, the *TOTP* theme 'Whole Lotta Love' was replaced by Phil Lynott's 'Yellow Pearl', which ran until 1986.

40. Culture Club made their *TOTP* debut because an act was needed at short notice to replace... Shakin' Stevens.

41. Don't laugh, ol' Shaky was the most successful UK chart act of the entire 1980s, mustering 30 hits including four No.1 singles.

42. And did Kevin Rowland *deliberately* have a huge photo of darts giant Jocky Wilson behind Dexy's Midnight Runners when they were on *TOTP* performing 'Jackie Wilson Said...'?

43. The Smiths appearance in November 1983 performing 'This Charming Man' is another of those iconic *TOTP* moments, mainly for Morrissey careering around with a bunch of gladioli.

44. On 3 October 1991 another seismic shift occurred, when all acts appearing on *TOTP* had to sing live...

45. The show's first stage invasion took place in November 1991, when an enthusiastic fan grabbed Kurt Cobain while Nirvana were performing 'Smells Like Teen Spirit'.

46. 31 October 1992 found OAP John Lee Hooker on with 'Boom Boom', making the 75 year-old blues giant the oldest performer on *Top of the Pops.*

47. *Top of the Pops 2* was launched in 1994 – "Top Of The Grand Pops" the press called it.

48. Celebrity *TOTP* presenters during the 1990s included Damon Albarn, Jarvis Cocker, Jack Dee, Angus Deayton, Jeremy Clarkson and Dale Winton.

49. The programme moved from Thursday evening to Friday night on BBC1, where it was head-to-head with *Coronation Street.*

50. Andrew Lloyd Webber was a surprise *TOTP* performer when he was on with Westlife performing a song from his *Whistle Down The Wind* musical.

51. In 2001, Jennifer Lopez made *Top of the Pops* history when she arrived with the biggest-ever entourage – 60.

52. In September 2002, Jamie Theakston presented the 2000th show, introducing N-Trance, Tom Jones & Wyclef Jean, Jurgen Vries, White Stripes, Atomic Kitten and Status Quo.

53. John Otway holds the record as the act with the longest gap between *Top of the Pops* appearances – 25 years between 1977's 'Really Free' and 2002's 'Bunsen Burner'.

54. In July 2005, after 41 years, the show switched channels from BBC 1 to BBC2 (which didn't even exist when *TOTP* began!)

55. The last-ever edition was broadcast on 30 July 2006, with a vintage show made of clips of everyone from the Rolling Stones to Gnarls Barkley; Sonny & Cher to Beyonce...

56. The glory of being the last act to perform live on a weekly edition of *Top of the Pops* was the penultimate show – Snow Patrol's 'Chasing Cars'.

57. In June 2013, Cadbury's conducted a survey to find out what the British public most wanted to make a comeback, and there in its rightful place, at No.1... was *Top of the Pops*!

BIBLIOGRAPHY

Buckley, David (2004) *The Thrill of it all: The Story of Bryan Ferry & Roxy Music* (Andre Deutsch).

Collins, Andrew (1998) *Billy Bragg: The Official Biography* (Virgin).

Devine, Campbell (1998) *Mott The Hoople: All the Young Dudes* (Cherry Red).

Geldof, Bob (1986) *Is That It?* (Sidgwick & Jackson).

Gittins, Ian (2007) *Top of the Pops: Mishaps, Miming & Music, True Adventures of TV's No.1 Pop Show* (BBC Books).

Harris, John (2003) *The Last Party* (4th Estate).

Hewitt, Paolo & Hellier, John *(2004) Steve Marriott: All Too Beautiful* (Helter Skelter).

Kutner, Jon & Leigh, Spencer (2005) *The 1000 UK Number One Hits* (Omnibus).

Lewisohn, Mark (1992) *The Complete Beatles Chronicle* (Pyramid).

Maconie, Stuart (1999) *Blur: 3862 Days* (Virgin).

McAleer, Dave, editor (2006) *British Hit Singles & Albums, 19th Edition* (Guinness World Records).

OFC (Official Charts Company) (2012) *The Million Sellers* (Omnibus).

Paytress, Mark (2002) *Bolan: The Rise & Fall of a 20th Century Superstar* (Omnibus).

Peel, John & Ravenscroft, Sheila (2005) *Margrave of The Marshes, The Autobiography* (Bantam).

Pegg, Nicholas (2011) *The Complete David Bowie* (Titan).

Povey, Glenn (2007) *Echoes: The Complete History of Pink Floyd* (Mind Head).

Rogan, Johnny (2005) *Van Morrison: No Surrender* (Secker & Warburg).

Simpson, Jeff (2002) *Top of the Pops, 1964–2002* (BBC Books).

Visconti, Tony (2007) *Bowie, Bolan & the Brooklyn Boy* (Harper Collins).

Wyman, Bill & Havers, Richard (2002) *Rolling with The Stones* (Dorling Kindersley).